D0901572

THE
DECISION
TO
HEAL

THE DECISION TO HEAL

PATHWAYS FROM SUFFERING TO LOVE

NICOLE SMITH   JOSH FRIEDBERG
JULIE RABORN   KRISTIN LARSEN
KATELYN M. FLORES   TERESA GRECO

gatekeeper press

Columbus, Ohio

The Decision to Heal: Pathways from Suffering to Love

Published by Gatekeeper Press
2167 Stringtown Rd, Suite 109
Columbus, OH 43123-2989
www.GatekeeperPress.com

The cover design, interior formatting, typesetting, and editorial work for this book are entirely the product of the author. Gatekeeper Press did not participate in and is not responsible for any aspect of these elements.

ISBN (hardcover): 9781642378269
ISBN (paperback): 9781642378276
eISBN: 9781642378283

To everyone who is suffering –
Know there is hope and you are not alone!

INTRODUCTION

Have you ever felt like what you had to say didn't matter? Or that it didn't have value? So instead you kept your dreams and aspirations quiet, because you thought no one would care to hear them anyway?

So many of my own dreams and visions have been lost over the years because I carried those same beliefs within myself.

But as things began to shift and change in my life, the visions that now come are so much stronger and harder to ignore. They are vivid and full of life; I feel them as though they have already happened... And this book in your hands is one of them.

Over the course of the past two years I have been on a personal growth journey that included taking the time to heal and find my voice. As I did, a crazy thing happened. The more I began to share about my personal challenges, the more I found others that were just like me. So many close and new friends said that they themselves kept their own pain hidden from others... but for the first time were finding strength and their own voices because of the realization that we all were never really alone. In fact, what we found was that thing that once isolated us was the very thing that brought us all together.

I have beautiful friends with their own powerful stories that all carry a common thread. That's when it hit me, the vision to create a collection of stories spreading the message we are not alone despite who we are, where we came from, or what we have been through. We are all united because our stories bond us in "The Decision to Heal."

—Nicole

****

Many people struggle with how to thrive in a world where the odds seem stacked against us.

Did you know that suicide is the tenth leading cause of death in the U.S.? In fact, 47,173 Americans died by suicide in 2017,[1] and in 2018 the U.S. military experienced the highest number of suicides among active duty personnel then it had over the last six years.[2]

I was shocked to hear that over 7.7 million adults are affected by Posttraumatic Stress Disorder (PTSD). Yes, you read that correctly, 7.7 MILLION! That is 3.5% of the United States population. What about the startling fact that depression is now the leading cause of disability worldwide!?![3]

The World Health Organization reports that 1 in 13 globally suffer from anxiety and it has become the most common mental disorder worldwide. A heartbreaking realization is that part of this statistic also includes the fact that 25% of children between the ages of 13-18 are also affected by anxiety.[4]

No wonder approximately 160,000 kids per day skip school for fear of being bullied, especially when statistics show that 1 in 3 students are in fact being bullied.[5] Since we are on the topic of children and bullying, sadly our, lesbian, gay, and bisexual youth are about five times as likely to have attempted suicide than heterosexual youth. And according to the National Center for Transgender Equality, two fifths of transgender adults reported that they have made a suicide attempt.[6]

According to the National Coalition against Domestic Violence, nearly 20 people per minute are physically abused by an intimate partner, that's 1 in 4 women and 1 in 9 men that are experiencing a severe form of abuse. So, it comes as no surprise that there is a link between intimate partner violence and depression and suicidal behavior.[7]

These are just some of the hard facts about the problems that many people around the world face every day. In a world like ours, hope can seem hard to come by. This is where we want to make a difference.

We are a group of coaches, writers, and thought leaders who came together to share our experiences of how we have worked through different issues to become stronger. Our stories cover issues of abuse, PTSD, depression, anxiety, bullying, Autism, personal insecurities, and other issues that affect many people daily. We are on a mission to share our stories in the hope that even one person, struggling somewhere with any hardship, can read our book and feel that there is hope.

For survivors of trauma, depression, anxiety, violence, assault, or any kind of hardship, the light at the end of the tunnel can appear dim, if it appears present at all. The belief we carry for ourselves, for you and everyone in this world, is that life truly is worth living—and that in a seemingly hopeless world things can get better.

Within this book you will find stories of hope, healing, and working through different obstacles to come to a better place in life. We don't claim to have all the answers, but we hope that our experiences show how attainable healing can be.

You didn't pick up this book by accident. If you're reading this, it's because you want something better for yourself . . . and because healing is possible for you. The vision we hold for you is that after reading these stories, you will be in a better place to work through any pain or trauma that you may have experienced. We have included six stories and a series of exercises, affirmations, and journal prompts at the end.

We want to provide readers with a resource that can assist in unlocking and uncovering the possibilities that are available in this moment.

Our hope for our readers is that this book will provide another viewpoint for choices, for possibility, for creating change in their lives, and even as a lifeline. We also hope that our workbook exercises, affirmations, and journal prompts can help enhance readers' healing. We want to hold a place for them to continue healing, growing, and learning while knowing they are not alone on their journey.

This book is a reminder you are not alone. Here we go! Let's do this!

THE PAIN WITHIN: NAVIGATING FROM SELF-HARM TO SELF-EMPOWERMENT

By: Nicole Smith

From inside the Coast Guard watch tower, I sat at the plexiglass-covered table, holding a pair of nautical plotting dividers, pushing the sharp needle end down into the table, mesmerized as I watched them twirl around and around. They reminded me of the mix of emotions flowing through my body. A warmth began spreading over my face, down my chest, and through my arms, causing my palms to slightly perspire. My heart pounded and ached as it dipped down into my chest and a tightness began to form in my throat, making it hard for me to swallow. I was overwhelmed by the weight of my emotions and the burden of holding onto all the regrets and pain.

My life that once seemed so happy and easy now felt like I had lost control. I was scared and didn't know how to handle it all.

"I just want it all to stop," I murmured to myself as I sat there. I didn't want to feel like this anymore, in fact, I didn't want to feel anything at all. I drove the needle end of the dividers into my arm. I felt everything all at once then, it quickly evaporated, and I was left with complete numbness. So numb that I didn't even feel the needle piercing into my forearm, nor did I realize what I was even doing until a bright red bead of blood dripped down onto the charting table.

The sight of my blood dripping down my arm, by my own hand, made me buzz with adrenaline. I felt a wave of relief wash over me as the feelings rush out. The physical sensation became a needed distraction for that moment of happiness to sneak in. For those few seconds, I was in control. All the sadness, self-loathing, anger, and betrayal I had been dealing with in the hours and days beforehand washed away, even if only temporarily. In that moment, everything else disappeared: the loss of two teenagers from a case we had a week prior, the problems with my new roommate, and the argument with my boyfriend the night before. It all went away, until it came back.

For as long as I can remember, I sought to fit in. I was desperate to be liked and I longed for connection. In my younger years, it wasn't such a hard thing to achieve. From preschool through eighth grade I attended a private Christian school, which had less than 300 students total, with only 18 in my graduating eighth grade class. Needless to say, my friends and environment didn't change much over my 10 years of attendance there. It was easy to fit in and even to be considered "popular" and "cool." I was very active and involved with school activities. In third grade I joined the choir and in the sixth grade I became a cheerleader. I was well-liked and friends with pretty much everyone, and for the most part we all got along. We never had any problems with bullying, fighting, or things of that nature that we associate with public schools these days. I suppose you could say it was because it wasn't part of the culture at a Christian School, but I am sure it also had a lot to do with its small size.

I don't think anything could have prepared me for high school. It was my first taste of a public school and boy, was I in for quite an awakening. I'd always heard that high school was where I was supposed to "find myself." My elementary friends and I went our separate ways, searching for and finding our own places and trying to discover who we wanted to be. I was coming from being at the top of the food chain in middle school to the very bottom in high school. All the other kids had gone to the public middle schools, which were so much larger than my whole school had been! So, they already had their own groups of friends and places of belonging that I was not a part of.

Dread and apprehension began settling in immediately once the school year began. Thoughts like, "Where do I belong?" "How am I supposed to fit in now when everyone else already seems too?" "Does anyone even see me?" were constant voices in my head. I was young and impressionable, so it wasn't long before I found myself following the lead of others to fit in. Then it happened. A few short months into my freshman year, I met my first love. His name was Landon and he was gorgeous—tall, athletic, with dark brown hair and eyes. He had a charm about him that drew everyone in. He was always the center of attention and always the person others chose to follow. He easily made conversation with anyone and was often cracking jokes and making everyone laugh.

Landon and I were in the same class and he sat one row over and a desk behind me. He had my attention and I am sure he knew it, but when his attention turned backed to me, I was ecstatic. I came to learn later that I initially caught his attention because he thought I looked smart and would be able to help him pass the class. Honestly, I think that even if I had known that, I would not have cared. I was in love. It was the kind of love that aches in your chest when you are not with the other person. It was a Romeo and Juliet kind of love, at least from my end.

We became inseparable. I wanted to be with him every second and I would have done anything to make him happy, and for the most part that's exactly what I did. I realize now, it never really was to make him happy, but rather, to make him stay with me. He always reminded me how lucky I was to have him and that when it came to me knowing him, or even how to please him, I hadn't even begun to scratch the surface. If only I had known the things I know now, I would have laughed in his face and told him to pack sand.

But of course, that is not how life works and obviously not how things happened, otherwise I wouldn't be here sharing my story with you. Instead, I found myself making decisions that left a familiar ache in my heart and which, to this day, I am not proud of. You may be thinking that I'm referring to common things like ditching school or sneaking out of my house and taking my family car to spend time with him. But honestly, even the act of losing my virginity was nothing compared to what I really lost subsequently.

We stayed together all four years of high school and then some. His friends became my friends, and soon I had my clique. Anything else that was once important to me was no longer a priority. I stopped doing things I truly enjoyed, like trying out for the school plays. I even dropped drama class from my sophomore year. Instead I picked up photography simply so I'd have a pass to roam the campus and be with him. I would regularly lie to my parents about where I was going or who I was with so that I could sneak away to meet up with him. My once perfect grades began to drop and my friendships and relationship with my parents began to suffer.

My junior year, my mom and I got into an explosive fight about my relationship with Landon. I had been working part-time at Claire's jewelry store after school and on the weekends. For a young teenage girl like me, it was the perfect job! It was like getting paid to shop—half my paycheck went back to them for all the jewelry, makeup, and accessories I bought. One of the weekends I was scheduled to work, Landon's family was out of town and he convinced me to call in sick so that we would have the whole weekend to hang out. So, I did. It seemed like the perfect cover because my parents assumed that I was at work all day. That was until my mom called the store to speak with me because she wanted me to pick something up on the way home, and much to her and my manager's surprise, I had lied to them both. Needless to say, my mom grounded me and I didn't work at the store much longer after that. I had assimilated to a life consumed by Landon. My world reflected him as my sole focus to the detriment of everything and everyone else. I had found what I thought I was looking for—connection and belonging—and even better, I had found love. And that love made me feel important and worthy. Nothing else mattered. I was blind and in my young mind, it was all for love, so that made it all okay.

During the few "breaks" we did take from being a couple, I would start talking to someone else, and it didn't take long for Landon to "get back at me" with belittling comments like, "Really, that guy?" or "Seriously, you are just embarrassing yourself." He would tell me that my male friends only wanted one thing from me, and that they didn't care about me as a friend; they didn't have my best interests at heart like he did. Maybe it was out of pity or his need for control, but we would always wind up back together, which was ultimately what I thought I wanted anyway. The only person I ever saw was Landon and he knew that. He controlled what I wore just by suggesting what I looked good in and what I didn't, how I styled my hair because of how sexy it looked on a girl that walked by, or the perfume I bought because he made sure I knew how sweet one of his female classmates smelled. Even when other guys were extremely kind and into me, I was still so preoccupied by Landon that they never stood a chance. As someone who had never had a serious boyfriend before and who was desperate for acceptance and belonging, I thought this was what it looked like when someone loves you—they want to control you. Because they care.

After graduation I was expecting to go off to college and looking forward to it. He was talking about finding work and staying nearby, but it's funny how quickly circumstances can change.

My plans for college fell through and my mom told me, "You better find something to do because you're not going to just sit on the couch all summer." So, finding something is exactly what I did.

As a graduation gift, my mom sent Landon and I to Catalina Island for the day.

We spent the warm summer day exploring and swimming, and we were sitting on the beach taking a break when he exclaimed, "Holy crap! Check that out."

He was pointing at a large white boat off in the distance with an orange helicopter hovering overhead.

"Who do you think that is?" I asked.

"I'm not sure, but I'm going to find out," he replied, while remaining fully captivated.

A week later, we were both sitting in a Coast Guard recruiting center. I listened while he asked questions.

Then the recruiter turned to both of us as he slid a piece of paper across the table and said, "You know, if you guys sign up together, I can put you on the buddy system. You'll go to boot camp at the same time and be stationed near each other, so you'll have familiar support." He handed us a pen and we both signed away. He shook our hands and gave us smile.

On the drive home, all I could think about was that I would be spending the summer with Landon and that we would never be too far from each other. I waited two days before I told my mom that I was leaving for boot camp and she wouldn't have to worry about me staying on the couch. She was shocked, but ultimately, I could tell she was happy because she had always wanted me to join ROTC and consider the military. A few days later, both of our families stood at the airport to say their good-byes and sent us off. The recruiter kept his word and we were off to boot camp together, assigned to the very same company, so we saw each other every day. Despite the problems in our relationship, it was extremely comforting to have someone I knew there; we could let the other know it was all okay and that we loved each other with just one look or hand gesture, like tugging on our ear.

The two months in bootcamp felt like forever, but finally, the day came when we received our assignments. Much to my disappointment, we did not get assigned near each other like our recruiter had promised. Instead, we were going to be over 500 miles apart. Despite Landon's attempt to console and assure me that we would drive and visit each other, I was heartbroken. Graduation came and went and before I knew it, I was checking into my first unit in the small coastal logging town of Coos Bay, Oregon. I reported in early November, which was in the midst of the rainy season and it was cold, foggy, and the sky was a dreary shade of grey. I had grown up in a small town in southern California in the middle of the Mojave Desert. I was used to hot ass summers and praying for rain. Now, here I was, in a rainy fishing community half the size of my hometown. I felt extremely out of place. Right on cue, all those old feelings came rushing back in like a tidal wave. "What have I gotten myself into?" I thought. "How the hell am I supposed to fit in here? What if no one likes me? What if I make a fool of myself, or don't get qualified? What if I let Mom down, Landon down, myself down?"

This was my first time away from home, and I was on my own. I was determined to make a good impression and really wanted to fit in. Because I was single and lower enlisted, I was assigned to the station barracks, which meant I would be sharing a room. At the time, only two other females lived on base and before I arrived had been lucky enough to have their own rooms. But now, I was going to make the third, which meant one of them was going to have to share with me. There were five girls assigned to the unit in total, but the other two were authorized to live off base. The barracks were located directly above the station, and I didn't own a car at the time, so I had no other choice but to stay close and focus on work.

As it turned out, the roommate assigned to me didn't sleep on base that often. So, when she requested to move off base, I was not the least bit surprised. It was nice to have my choice to a side of the room and I decided to take the bed by the window. Other than my dresser from home and a government-assigned locker, I didn't have much. On my dresser I kept a few pictures of my family and of Landon and me. The window of my room faced out to the station's boat house and local marina. Most mornings I would wake up to sounds of barking seals stretched out on the boat docks across from the parking lot below.

I was only alone in the room for a few months before a new girl reported and was assigned as my roommate. Initially, I was so excited about having another girl onboard and was hopeful that we would become friends. But only a few days after her arrival, I began having reservations about her. She was loud, obnoxious, and loved making crude jokes about some of the other girls. She was often disrespectful to our supervisors, but she had a charm about her that made it easy for her to talk her way out of anything. So, nothing was ever really done about it.

My roommate and I were the youngest females assigned to the station. I was 18 and just six months out of Coast Guard boot camp. I took the job seriously and worked hard to become a fully qualified member of my unit. For a member of my ranking, I was required to qualify as the station's radio watch stander, a tower watch stander, and a small boat crewman. Each of these jobs had their perks, but because of the uniqueness of our station, I loved getting underway on our small boats. My station was one of 21 Surf Boat Stations in the Coast Guard. Surf Stations are in areas where the ocean waves are greater than eight feet high and come close to shore before breaking, creating dangerous boating conditions. Our station was located on the treacherous Oregon coast and had an entrance bar that when breaking was known to be narrow and dangerous. To ensure our crews were always prepared for any situation, there wasn't a day that we weren't out in the breaking surf training. Three of our lifeboats were specifically built for the weather we often endured on the coast and could withstand the most severe conditions at sea.

One weekend while I was on duty, the station received notification over the radio that two teenage boys had been hit by what locals referred to as a "sneaker wave." These unforgiving and massive waves unexpectedly rush ashore, washing away anything in its path. They are a sobering reality, sometimes coming three in a day and other times weeks could go by without a single one. I was assigned as a boat crewman that day and my boat crew plus another response boat were launched immediately to respond to the search area where the boys had last been seen. After an extensive search, the other lifeboat recovered one of the boys and reported over the radio that he was unresponsive. They returned to the station where the young boy was pronounced dead on arrival. My crew stayed out and continued to search tirelessly into the evening and again the following morning for the other boy. Our Commanding Officer, or Skipper as we referred to him, informed us prior to going out that morning that due to the nature of the situation, the offshore weather conditions, and sea temperatures, we were shifting from an active search and rescue case to a recovery case.

It was the first time I ever had to face the fact that I may be seeing a dead body, and I didn't know if I could handle it. It seemed like my crewmates were unfazed by this news, but I, on the other hand, was panicking. The only time I had ever seen a dead body was at a funeral after it had been carefully preserved. I tried picturing my own wrinkly fingers after a long day of swimming as if to prepare myself only to become distracted by thoughts of what he might look like after days in the frigid ocean waters.

As embarrassed as I am to say this, I was a bit relieved when we were unable to find him that day. I was nowhere near ready at that young age to deal with something so traumatic. On the third morning of the case, my duty section was relieved by the oncoming duty section. During our morning muster with the Skipper, we were informed that local law enforcement had located the missing boy's body, which had washed up on shore. I shuddered as a chill came over me. I couldn't help but feel guilty. What if my thoughts kept me from doing my job well enough? Had I inadvertently given up? Was his death all my fault? I completely shut down and couldn't speak. When the Skipper asked if anyone wanted to talk with the chaplain, I just shook my head no. How could I dare share with anyone about how I was feeling, let alone allow my fellow shipmates to see I couldn't handle it? Most have them had years of experience and were experts at leaping into action at the sound of the search and rescue alarm without much consideration to their personal feelings or state of mind. They were conditioned and well-trained to deal with real life and death issues every day. So, as they all turned down the support, so did I.

I became so angry at myself for feeling relieved that my crew hadn't found him. Many nights I would wake up drenched in sweat, startled by a nightmare of us finding him and me pulling his lifeless, wet, cold and decomposing body out of the water. Even now when I find myself in situations where I feel I didn't do well enough or have let somebody down, this dream will still haunt me.

A week after the boy was found, a few of my shipmates must have sensed that I was a little reserved because they invited me to go out to town and hang out with them. Still trying to adjust to life in the military, I wanted nothing more than to make a good name for myself and fit in, so I was more than happy to tag along that night. Little did I know that going out for a much-needed evening to decompress and have some fun would result in my world being tossed upside down.

While I was out that night, Landon called the station to speak to me and my new roommate picked up the call. Now let me paint a clear picture for you here. This was before everyone had cell phones and we did not have personal phone lines in the barracks. When someone called, they had to call into the stations main line and ask for the person they wanted to speak to. The watch stander would then place them on hold, make a page over the station's intercom system, and announce that someone had a call holding on x, y, z line for them. We then would pick up the nearest phone, dial in the extension, and the call was transferred to us. So rather than allowing the watch stander to do their job and take a message for me, my roommate decided to answer my phone call. And, rather than politely taking a message or letting him know I would be back shortly, I later found out that she told him I was out with a group of guys that I had been known to flirt with and "God only knows" what we were out doing. She told him I had been trying to hook up with one of my coworkers. She told him she didn't even know I had a boyfriend until now, even though pictures of us covered my dresser and I talked about him all the time. I had witnessed her lewd behavior with the guys around the station, but I never thought I had to be concerned about my own boyfriend, who lived 500 miles away.

I returned to my barracks room that evening to find a hand-scribbled note on my dresser saying, "You should probably give Landon a call he seems pretty upset. P.S. He's got a sexy voice." Over the course of a two-hour conversation with him, she had managed to finally destroy my already-rocky five-year relationship. It had been stressful enough trying to hold it together long distance without having to defend myself, my whereabouts, and my choice of friends.

I called him back that night and was immediately berated with comments like, "It was only a matter of time before I knew you would become like all the other girls," and using an infamous military term meaning a piece of ass, referring to me as "Just another piece of morale gear." My voice shook and chin quivered as I begged him to just listen and let me explain, but he wouldn't have it. Instead he interjected, "Your roomie seems like a pretty hot chick, why don't you help a brother out and hook me up?" My whole body began shaking as hysterical sobs coursed through my body, leaving me barely able to respond. "I love you Landon, please," I was finally able to mumble.

"You brought this upon yourself, Ni-co-co," he countered back with his once endearing nickname for me. The next thing I heard was the dial tone.

The phone dropped from my hand. I found it hard to breathe and while my heart began to race, it simultaneously felt like it was being yanked from my chest. I was dizzy and my stomach was churning. I didn't know it then, but I was having my first of what would be many panic attacks. The only thing I knew in that moment as the room began to fade away was that I felt like I was dying. Call it luck or maybe divine intervention, but Melissa, the girl who was assigned to the room next to mine, happened to be grabbing something from her room and heard my sobs. When I didn't respond to her knock at the door, she entered my room and ran over when she saw me lying on the floor. Sadly, I hadn't made a point to get to know her. When I had first reported, one of the girls had warned me to stay away from her because she was "trouble."

But as Melissa lifted my head and put it in her lap she whispered, "Just Breathe". In that moment, I could not for the life of me figure out why people thought of her that way.

The next morning, I woke up like I had many others before, to the seals barking and the sound of revile playing through the speaker mounted on the wall of my barracks room. Only, it wasn't like any other morning. On this morning, I felt nearly broken. I rolled out of bed, slowly making my way to the bathroom, mechanically showering, brushing my teeth, and pulling back my wet hair into a tightly rolled bun. I dressed in my uniform then sat on the edge of my bed to lace up my freshly polished boots. I made my way downstairs to the station's watch room to find my assignment for the day. I was relieved to see I had been assigned the first watch up in the station's lookout tower. It was a place where I could be alone and not have to answer a million questions as to why I looked so sad or why my eyes were blood shot. Most days, I loved making the drive up to the tower with the stereo on and the windows rolled down in the station's big blue Chevy. It was a fun drive up the gravel cut road with winding turns, large drop offs and an aroma of large cedar, fir and spruce trees. At the top, the narrow tree-lined road opened to a large clearing that overlooked the rocky Pacific coast. The combination of high elevation and vast openness provided the tower with an unobstructed 360-degree view of the Coos Bay entrance channel, the rugged coastline below, and quiet little fishing town behind in the distance. Despite the relief I felt for my watch tower assignment, I was still hovering above a total breakdown. The drive was filled with silence and I took no notice to the lush surroundings.

As a qualified tower watch stander, my job was to monitor the sea state and bar conditions and determine if it was too dangerous to allow both commercial and recreational boaters passage in and out of the bay. Any time one of our station boats were under way, it was also my responsibility to be their lookout, ensuring they made it across the bar safely and provide reports back to my station. Most days, it was a pretty relaxing duty and I was able to enjoy the beautiful sunrise and sunsets. Some evenings, I could see more stars than my mind could even fathom existed.

While I climbed up the ladder of the two-story structure that morning, I could hardly hold back my tears. As I entered the tower, a strong aroma of musty carpet caused by the salty air and sea spray infiltrated my nose. With a small gasp and a cough, I held back from releasing the tears brimming up in my eyes. I had a job to do. I flicked on the radios, grabbed the binoculars, and made my way back out to the observation deck. I took in a deep breath while I scanned the horizon and evaluated the sea state. It was a clear day despite it being overcast and damp, and there was only one vessel in sight many miles offshore. I made one more scan of the horizon and proceeded back inside. I reached for the large army green record book and made my entry into the tower's watch log, then relayed my observation report back to the stations watch stander.

As I sat at the large charting table, looking out at the dull grey sky and crashing waves below, I reached for the plotting dividers that were sitting at the edge of the table and twirled them around. It was in that moment, after all that had happened in the past few weeks, that I felt I had no other choice but to drive the needle end into my skin. I had never hurt myself before and never imagined I would ever take to such an extreme, but it happened, and I was comforted by its distraction.

Underneath the table was a large roll of brown commercial grade paper towels. I tore off a piece and held it tightly to my arm, closing my eyes as I winced from the throbbing that now pulsed from the wound. Underneath the table was also a small first aid kit and a bottle of Simple green that we used to clean pretty much everything. I found a small band aid in the kit and used it to cover the site of the puncture. Then, I lightly sprayed the highly concentrated cleanser onto the chart table and dividers, the air instantly filling with a pungent mixture of pine and mint. I scrubbed down the table and wiped off the dividers, careful to clean up any evidence of what I'd done. Then I placed the dividers into the table drawer where they belonged and put away the cleaning gear. I glanced down at my watch and was shocked that 45 minutes had gone by. I had to be back at the station in 10 minutes to provide relief for the other watch stander to have lunch. I made one more final scan of the water way, phoned in my last report, locked up, and made my way out of the tower.

A few of the guys were standing outside talking and laughing as I pulled back into the station. One of them was with the group I had gone out with the night before; he waved and gestured for me to join them as I hopped out of the truck.

"Hey! I'm glad you came out with us last night," he said as I made my way over.

"Uh, yea. It was fun," I said softly.

Noticing how quiet I was, he gently nudged my arm with his and asked, "You doing alright? I know it's been a crazy week."

Rubbing over the newly placed band aid, I nodded and replied with a forced smile, "Yea, yea I'm Fine."

"That's good to hear. You are really settling in well and doing a great job around here. It's been a while since we had someone as hard working as you," he said.

As I began to turn and walk away, I really wanted to believe him. I was almost through the station door when I heard him yell, "It will get easier, I promise. Just hang in there and keep up the good work." My eyes began to sting from the tears forming in my eyes as the door closed behind me. I made my way through the station and up to my room, allowing myself to freshen up and splash water on my face before going back down to relieve my shipmate for lunch.

On the outside, I may have looked like the girl who was settling in at work and happy most of the time. But my persona didn't align with what I was feeling on the inside. Inside, a war was just beginning, and a new cycle of self-inflicted physical pain became my distraction from the emotional pain I couldn't seem to escape.

After that day, I stopped trying to be friends with everyone at the station. In fact, I really only became good friends with one—Melissa. The girl I once judged based on what I heard from others was the only one I felt didn't judge me. Melissa never pressed me for details of what happened that night in my room. Instead she took me under her wing and became one of the few good friends I had while stationed in Oregon. Over time, with her help, I collected the pieces of me that had shattered that night.

That fight with Landon was not just our biggest, it was also our last. I tried to escape the heartache of our break-up by burying myself in work but unfortunately, life at the station got harder before it got better. The bullying and rumors from my roommate continued for months after. There was just no escaping her; I had to work, eat, and pretty much sleep beside this girl 24/7, because we weren't just roommates, we were co-workers too.

Melissa helped me build up the courage to report a complaint against her to my command. When they approached her to get her side of the story, my commanding officer and supervisor saw right through her lies. Before I had reported to the station, Melissa had put in a request to move out of the barracks, but it was denied. But now, because of my complaint, the command approved Melissa's request and they moved my roommate into Melissa's old room, allowing me to have my room to myself again. What made things even better was that they even moved her to the opposite duty section where she ended up meeting and dating one of the guys she worked with, so I never had to see her because she stopped sleeping on base. I was so relieved that my command completely supported me and my request.

If there's one thing that Melissa's friendship has taught me, it's that our friends and the people we surround ourselves with have a tremendous influence on our beliefs and actions. The need I had for connection and belonging was so intense it created within me a fear of being ostracized by others. I wound up compromising my own values, wants, needs and beliefs as a sacrifice to pleasing those around me. Only the more I pleased and gave into others, the worse I was treated and the more miserable I felt. As cliché as it may sound, I learned to never judge a book by its cover. This lesson grew along with me as I transitioned my way not only through the military but also through life. Ultimately, the final lesson learned was: Genuine connection and belonging comes from staying true to who you are, what you believe in and following your own moral compass, even in the foggiest of conditions.

In early 2001, I packed up my belongings and said good-bye to my first Coast Guard unit. I received orders to telecommunications school and transferred to Petaluma,

California. As fate would have it, Landon had also received orders to Petaluma and was there for his own specialized training. We bumped into each other a few times at the chow hall or making our way through the halls of the barracks. On a few occasions he even had the nerve to show up at my room looking to "hang out." However, I wasn't as weak anymore and didn't cave into his charming ways. Instead, I focused on graduating and making new friends. After successfully completing training, I received my advancement and orders to a Communications Station not far from the school. Landon graduated from school a few months later and transferred to a station once again hundreds of miles away. This time, we finally went our separate ways. I focused on work, advanced quickly, and went on to create a successful career for myself.

However, the same cannot be said about my life outside of work. I found myself back in a place of just wanting and needing to be loved, even if that feeling came from the occasional one-night stand. I was in and out of relationships, never taking a moment to catch my breath in between. The bar was set low and I found myself in relationships that were abusive, bullying, and obsessive. I wound up dating a guy from work named Owen. We shared a lot of the same interests and enjoyed each other's company. Whether it was pizza and movie nights at his place or road trips up to the redwoods on his motorcycle, we always had a lot fun. He had great work ethic; he even had a side job to save for his future. He planned to become a cop after his enlistment was up and some of our dates were spent by me helping him study. He made me feel safe and taken care of.

Until one afternoon I went out to the movies with a few of my friends while he was at work and I missed his calls. When I pulled up to my house, Owen was there waiting at my front door. He was furious! From then on, he demanded to know my every movement and would limit who I was friends with and how much time I got to hang out with them. He started throwing things when I made him upset. Once, when a girlfriend of mine was in need of a friend, I refused to stay home with him, so he threw a drinking glass at my car as I drove away. Another time he threw his keys at my head because he didn't believe me when I told him where I had been. All of this finally began to affect my work. Seldomly we would wind up being scheduled to work the same rotation and one night, in a jealous fit of rage, he punched a wall because I had been talking to my supervisor rather than focusing my attention on him.

I finally found the courage to end the relationship when I received orders to move across country. But the cycle was far from over and I fell right into another relationship. This time, it was with an old friend I had once been stationed with. Jacob had left the military to try and work on his marriage but shortly after he did, she filed for divorce. We were both on the rebound so right off that bat, we were in it for all the wrong reasons. Within a few months of dating, Jacob left his job and home and moved in with me. He had two adorable kids that lived with his ex-wife back in his hometown.

Prior to leaving California, I had re-enlisted for another four years of service and received a large monetary bonus.

It didn't take long before Jacob and I had completely blown through it to cover the costs of all the trips we'd take so he could see his kids. When we were there, he would constantly compare me to his ex, which made me feel inadequate. He wanted me to be involved with his kids but anytime I would say something to them, he would contradict me. Back home, I would drive over an hour in traffic to get home after working a 12-hour shift to find a mess and him demanding dinner. We started arguing about everything, but money and his children became the most common.

During a momentary high, Jacob convinced me that everything would be better if we got married. He said that I would make more money by having a dependent, he would have medical coverage, the list went on and on. It seemed like a logical decision at the time, but I have come to learn that logical doesn't always mean right. All alone on a cold January day, we got married by justice of the peace. The only people who knew were the administrative staff at my work so I would start to receive my married benefits. It killed me keeping a secret that big from our families.

After that, he became more and more controlling. When it came time for my next assignment, he demanded I take the location closer to his hometown even though it wasn't a position I desired, but I went with it anyway. We were there only a few months before he started driving home on the weekends so he could go visit his parents and kids. During my first deployment I received emails from Jacob saying that he was going to move home while I was gone and would return when I got back. Then the next one said he was moving back to his hometown permanently but would visit me on my days off. Next came the crude comments, flashing me back to my argument with Landon, about what woman are like in the military and writing things like, "You better not become a piece of moral gear," or "Hope you are behaving yourself out there." I couldn't take it anymore. This was not how I envisioned my marriage to be. Somewhere deep within me, I found the strength to tell him I was leaving. I didn't get a response until I returned home to find an empty house. After only nine months of marriage, I filed for divorce and five months later it was finalized. He didn't even show up for the hearing.

During our marriage, I stopped putting in as much effort at work and forgot what I loved about the Coast Guard. I took the next few months to re-focus on work and find my ability to lead. I was reminded of my independence and began developing a strong sense of self without a man by my side. When I finally met my now husband, Luke, I experienced a different kind of love. He was loving me and wanting me like I had always desired, but it was only after I had found that love and belonging within myself first.

Six years later and just four months before the birth of my first son, I was sent to a specialized training in Virginia. To my surprise, I crossed paths with Landon one more time. We agreed to have dinner and catch up. We started off with casual conversation about the Coast Guard and where we had been stationed since last seeing each other. He asked about my obvious baby bump and I shared that I had recently gotten married. I learned that he had been married too, but during one of his deployments, she cheated on him and that he was now divorced. I am not exactly sure what came over me, but I mumbled under my breath, "What goes around, comes around," loud enough for him to hear me. I was just as surprised that I said it as he was. I didn't regret saying it, but rather found myself straightening up in my seat and looking him dead in the eyes.

"Well, that is a pretty harsh thing to say," he said. What came next was a flood of everything I had been holding onto for years. I reminded him of all that we had been through together, how much he had hurt me and what that pain had led too. I wasn't expecting him to say anything in response, but he acknowledged everything and even apologized for the person he was back then and for hurting me. I received something that night that not very many will ever get - closure. The hole that had been in my heart for years closed as I not only found my voice, but I found healing. As a testament to both of us and all that we had gone through together and the growing up we had done during the years apart, we were able to be adults and have remained good friends to this day. While I decided to make a career of my military service, Landon wound up leaving the Coast Guard, moved back to the west coast, and was lucky to catch the eye of an amazing and beautiful woman.

As for me, Luke and I have been married for 13 years now and are raising three venturous young boys. We originally met while assigned to the same ship in the Coast Guard, and because our friendship had given the perception that we were dating (which wasn't allowed), I got in trouble for being in an inappropriate relationship. Luke got orders off the boat and we wound up officially dating. We were together for about a year and half when we found out we

THE DECISION TO HEAL

were pregnant and decided to get married. Our relationship hasn't always been roses, and he will surely attest to that, but I try to work through old habits of wanting to give up. Luckily, he loves me for me and all the baggage I bring to the table. He has stuck by my side, calls me on my bullshit, and anchors me while I worked through my past to find closure and my voice. He was my number one supporter when I made the decision to retire from the Coast Guard and pursue life coaching. He understands the passion inside me and relates in his own way to the power of turning our "mess into a message." This is where my story comes full circle. I have come to believe in the importance of sharing our stories, to provide hope for others that they, too can find belonging, and inspire them to find peace and freedom.

Years after I began healing and finding my sense of self-love, I discovered just how much my story has impacted the type of mother I am today. On my birthday, May 18th, 2018, instead of celebrating… tragedy struck, when a 17-year-old boy shot and killed 10 of his classmates at Santé Fe High School in Texas. News of the shooting traveled fast. Everyone around me was talking about it and there wasn't a TV I passed that didn't have the news blaring with constant updates. I didn't know any of the victims personally. In fact, I didn't know any of the students or teachers at all. But that didn't matter. I was shaking and became frantic for all those impacted, including my own children, who were on alert in an elementary school nearby.

My kids came home from school that day asking questions that as a parent we never think we will have to answer and pray to never have to talk about. That afternoon, I sat with my boys answering questions about why their teachers were crying and why they had been locked inside their classrooms. It broke my heart to be sitting with my young, elementary school-aged boys having these adult conversations. The intensity of my sadness in those moments was all too familiar; inexplicably, my mind flashed back to the euphoria I had once felt driving a needle into my arms. Despite the tragedy of the situation, I found myself empathizing with that 17-year-old boy because I, too, had done dark, violent things to deal with my emotional pain. Only I had done them to myself and not others. I could only imagine the suffering he could have been feeling to take such horrific action.

After seeing the devastating news on TV, a good friend of mine called to check on us. The first words out of her mouth were: "That bastard, look at all the pain that he has caused." I gripped tightly to the phone as my jaw dropped. Taken back from her comment, a piercing pain stabbed deep within my chest. I thought again of that morning in the tower with the dividers piercing into my arm. I knew the depth of pain it had taken to inflict harm upon myself, and I understood that the pain came from a deeply rooted longing for connection and to be loved.

Instead of agreeing with my friend, my mind went to sympathizing with that poor child. What secret burdens did he carry that caused so much pain that he made the decision that day to walk into his school, open fire and take the lives of others? Was he also desperately longing to feel loved? Had he ever been abused? Was he being bullied? I thought back to my roommate who harassed me, the boyfriends that abused me and that's when it hit me. Hurt people—hurt people. Maybe my roommate had been struggling herself to fit in and the only way she knew how to prove herself was in an overbearing way. Or, what if my boyfriends had once felt abandoned, so their actions towards me were because they were terrified to end up alone?

I couldn't help but wonder, had this young 17-year-old boy been ignored or made to feel lost, abandoned, unworthy, not good enough? In the past, I would have backed into a dark place from her comment, but this time was different. I had been working with a life coach for the past year and was nine months into my journey of becoming a life coach myself. I had found someone who provided me with a safe space to share all that I had been through without a fear of judgment or embarrassment. I was surprised to find that the more I opened up, the stronger I felt and the more comfortable I was sharing my story with others. All my old wounds were closing and the limiting beliefs I had been holding onto were being replaced with ones of compassion and positivity.

So, instead of shutting down or snapping back at her remark, I challenged her. "Erica, we have no idea what this boy has been through. We don't know the pain, trauma, or experiences that may be behind his degenerated decision today."

She apologetically responded, "You are so right. I'm sorry I said it and sorry if I hurt you. I appreciate you helping me to see it in another light."

It was in that moment that something within me shifted and changed forever the conversations I had with those close to me. Already having begun to speak up about my own mental health, starting to find the strength and wanting to make an impact, another piece of me began to heal.

Later that night, my sons were upstairs playing in the loft and I heard my youngest son call to his brothers a few times with no response. Soon after, they all started yelling, arguing over a toy that my youngest wanted to play with. He was being abnormally mean and aggressive. So, when my older two ran into my office to tattle, I got up and took them back into the living room and asked them to all sit down with me. We sat on the floor in a circle with our legs crossed so that we could all look at each other.

"What is Brett doing that has you both upset?" I asked of my older boys.

"He's hitting us," Peyton, my oldest said, almost yelling.

"He's being mean and taking stuff," added Colin, the middle of my three boys.

"Okay, Okay. Why is he being mean and hitting you guys?" I asked. "I understand what he's doing, but I want you to tell me why he's doing it," I added.

I sat quietly, waiting for their response. When neither Peyton or Colin responded, I reached for their hands and explained, "Guys, I heard Brett calling your names over and over, but neither of you answered him. He's hitting you and throwing things because he's wanting your attention. He wants to play with you and do what you guys are doing." We talked about how younger brothers look up to their big brothers, and believe they are cool and special. It made sense that Brett wanted to play with them, he wanted to be included and be cool too. I told them that when I was included in things it made me feel important, special, and that I was liked. I could see the wheels turning and knew it was making sense to them. "Do you feel important, special and liked?" I asked them all.

"Yes, Momma." All of them nodded their heads.

That's when it hit me. I had a difficult decision to make. I could have either let them go back to playing and hope they understood, or I could take this opportunity to talk to my children about the impact of bullying and a person's need for connection. With the combination of my past, the events of that day, and the conversation with Erica, I chose the latter.

I told Brett to go on and play, and I pulled Peyton and Colin in closer. They were 10 and 8 at the time and unfortunately had both already been victims of bullying at school.

Looking Peyton in the eyes, I asked, "How did you feel when you were called spackle face and ugly just because you have freckles on your face?"

The question brought him to tears. "I was sad, and I got upset." Focusing over to Colin, I asked him, "What did it feel like when you got pushed into the fence at school?"

Looking down at his hands he answered, "Sad. He hurt my feelings. I don't understand why I couldn't play with them."

Nodding my head in understanding, I pushed on. I offered for them to consider, "What if when those boys are at home, in a place that you know to be fun and safe, theirs are not?" They looked up at me inquisitively. I spoke about how some family homes children are made fun of and called names like ugly, stupid and worthless, while other kids may be abused by the people, they should be able to trust. But instead, they are pushed by their brothers, punched by their fathers, or locked away in a room alone by their mothers. I shared with them that mommy had been hurt in her past by people she had loved and trusted and allowed it to happen because I didn't understand that it was wrong, and that how they treated me was not an act of love. They listened while I told them that some people unfortunately don't know what love and kindness look like, so instead, their way of finding attention is by lashing out on those around with them with the same behaviors that have been taken on them.

So, when these kids come to school, I explained, they often pick on the kids smaller than them. They are looking for a way to take out their anger and frustration, to release the pain and the bitterness they deal with daily, and unfortunately school has become the place they have found to do that. Their bullying has become their way to manage what they have been exposed to. At this point, all three of us were in tears.

Throughout our conversation, I kept thinking back to the experience with my roommate and wondered how I may have handled the situation differently. What if instead of wanting nothing more than to get away from her and blame her, I had drawn her in and befriended her? What if I had just challenged her behavior and attempted to tear down the walls of her "I have to be tough" exterior? Imagine the difference it could have had for the both of us. It was from this space that I spoke from to my children that day.

I might upset some of the parents reading this, but I saw it as an opportunity to make a difference in the lives of my children. I wanted them to be armed with the understanding that while yes, there are people who just do bad things in the world for no reason, there are also good people who do hurtful things to others from their own place of being sad and hurt. Unfortunately, because of the shifts in our society, as a parent I constantly worry about the violence and bullying that are now normal in our kid's schools. All these things we once hardly ever heard of in our own childhoods are becoming frequent occurrences and almost creating a sense of complacency, of normalcy, and they shouldn't be!

Not only that, but in the mind of so many, we want to place blame on the aggressor. We want answers. We want justice. We want to get to the bottom of it. All too often, though, we discover that something in the aggressor's past had provoked them to a moment of so much pain. In many cases, if someone had noticed their pain earlier, it would have been talked about and situations like this could have been prevented.

I have learned through the years that what you are silent about, you become bitter about. What we deal with internally, what we struggle with every day, the battles we fight with every day, all come from experiences we are not talking about. For myself, I stayed silent about being lonely and feeling that I wasn't worthy or good enough for people. I believed that I wasn't capable of being loved and all that internalization led to my battle with anxiety, depression and desire to self-harm. There were even times when thoughts of suicide crossed my mind; it is a growing epidemic that isn't talked about enough. Too many people are suffering in silence and believe their only way out of the pain, anger and frustration is to take their life.

Having that conversation with Erica and my sons that evening, I decided I would no longer stay silent. I want to be a voice not only for myself and for my children, but for so many out there that have yet to find their own. So many people are being bullied, maybe not even outwardly, but internally. Perhaps they have wounds we can't see and they criticize and beat themselves up every single day. They hold shame. They hold doubt. They hold fear and embarrassment, and all that weighs down on them.

By sharing my story, I have not only found my voice, strength, and community, but I've realized I was never truly alone. I had myself all along. I have found a group of like-minded friends, my fellow authors to be exact, and we have come together around a wild idea to share our stories in hopes of proving to others like you, that you too are never alone. Instead, I want you to know there are others out there that will rally around you, that will lock arms with you and help you rise just like I have found. Don't settle for anything less. You deserve people by your side who inspire you, love you and support you! You deserve to know you are not any of the things you once believed about yourself. Instead I hope you can one day believe this for yourself. Until then, I will believe enough for all of us—that you are loved, you are worthy, you do have a place in this world, and you really do matter.

THE FIGHTER STILL REMAINS: A STORY OF CREATIVITY, METAPHORS, AND TRIUMPH

By: Josh Friedberg

"**W**hat's wrong?" I asked a perturbed student during my eleventh-grade math class.

"You existed," he responded, seemingly thinking that was a good punchline.

I remember the feeling of helplessness and the shiver in my skin as I turned my head away from the bully. I didn't want to react to someone who easily could have kicked my ass. The school building was decrepit, the administration and teachers were (mostly) complacent, and the other students were (mostly) indifferent. Had I gone to a public school, the bullying could have been worse. I was, in many ways, extremely lucky. I went to a private school on a four-year full tuition merit scholarship that I applied for in eighth grade as a "distinguished scholar."

But that doesn't mean that what I went through wasn't abuse. My mother once told a sympathetic teacher, "The bravest thing that my son does every day is get up and go to school." The teacher agreed.

Something about silence has always bothered me. Not because I'm a talkative person, but because for most of my life, having to remain silent meant that I wasn't safe. It meant keeping my mouth shut in the face of verbal abuse.

I am grateful I didn't die in high school, or in the first 18 years of my life, period. For years, bullies treated me like I was worthless, whether by verbally provoking me because they knew I was sensitive or by humiliating me in other ways. One time in sixth grade, two bullies pulled my shorts down in the hall after gym class, which I responded to by crying. But after that, I mostly responded by remaining silent, trying not to give them the benefit of a reaction.

Even seemingly painless things felt significant in the larger context of how others treated me. For example, when I was 17 years old, I was in a small choir and one person constantly badgered me about how to sing. This became intensely irritating because of their repetition. In that situation, no matter how much rage I felt, I kept my head down and did my best to not react because I realized it wouldn't do any good at a school where I had just about no allies. Another person in that choir later told me, "I couldn't take it," watching me being treated so terribly with no recourse.

I tried to bring my silence home by not telling my family or others about what was going on. But I found out later that it was obvious to everyone that I was being treated like my concerns and my life didn't matter. I must have come home seeming pretty damn dejected every day.

Every so often, although rarely, my anger would erupt at school. I would explode by yelling at people. One time, I threw a flashlight at a bully who wouldn't leave me alone; I don't remember what he said, but he was constantly provoking me because he knew that he could get a rise out of me. It hurt so much to be so consistently misunderstood and abused because I was different.

I later found out that during high school, multiple people had felt like they couldn't take seeing me being treated like crap with nothing being done about it. They later said it had been obvious to everyone that I was suffering. I had thought these people had no idea what was going on, but I learned that some of them were engaging in their own maladaptive behaviors to cope with witnessing the ferocity of bullying that was happening to me. Some people told me they dealt with it by binge eating their brains out, including by overeating at social events. They were literally stuffing their feelings inside with junk food.

When I found that out, I remember feeling something like, "Wow, I guess it really did suck." It was validating to learn how those bullies had affected others, not just me. I wasn't overreacting. I wasn't being too sensitive. I was legitimately treated like shit in an environment that enabled kids to get away with vicious bullying. It doesn't matter that it was "only" verbal abuse; I was still made to feel like I shouldn't exist because I was different. For an impressionable, hyper-literal Autistic kid who was dealing with all kinds of social challenges, including navigating being gay, that mattered.

The day before my high school graduation, I came home from the awards ceremony, where I had won a number of academic and extracurricular honors, and cried because I realized that what I had really craved—social validation—was unattainable. No matter how many other students had signed nice comments in my yearbook, I cried because I realized I had not made one real, close friend in four years. My mother was sitting there next to me, but I couldn't stop crying.

Looking back, I try not to blame those kids for what they did, nor do I blame myself for being different. I was hyper-anxious and openly obsessive about things other kids didn't care about. I have, however, blamed the environment that allowed bullies to get away with the perpetuation of cruelty. Then again, at this point, the quality of my anger and the quantity of people towards whom I feel anything close to rage have substantially decreased. That is a miracle, and it took a lot of work.

Years after college, I reconnected with one of the few people who was remotely nice to me in high school. He tried to explain to me that no one hated me in high school. I then made a reference to how shitty I was treated for the first 18 years of my life and how it hurt others, and his response was, "It's just a word," referring to "faggot," "retard," "pussy," "prick," and other words that were hurled at me for years.

To my credit, I said nothing in response. This was extraordinary given that I was dealing with medication-induced mania and pressured speech, which meant I was talking and strongly reacting to people more than ever

before. That's saying something because despite the importance of silence in my life, I've always loved to talk. I wanted
to lecture him about privileged ignorance; as far as I know,
the person who made that comment is a heterosexual white
male who was unaware of how language has very much
hurt marginalized and oppressed peoples over the centuries.

Although my anger about past incidences has largely
subsided, I still do not owe anyone any explanation for why
I care so much about how people use words. I believe that
if you don't care about the words people choose to use,
you might have some privilege you're not acknowledging.
Yes, I have plentiful privilege in terms of being white, male,
and middle class. However, I'm also Autistic and gay, and
words matter to me. I am more sensitive because of my
Autism, which is to say that I am never "too sensitive" for
caring about words like "faggot" and "retard."

For most of my life to date, I felt that my struggles
against both external and internalized hate and misunderstanding, especially with language, defined my life. They
don't anymore. And this is not just because the external
circumstances have changed.

As a kid, for a time, it seemed like luck was on my side,
especially because I was born on the beautifully even date of
8-8-88 (August 8, 1988). I'm told that as a baby, I was calm.
But as a four-year-old, there was a sharp turn where I became
violent. I was kicking, screaming, hitting, biting, and verbally
abusing my mother, and I didn't know how to interact with
peers. I remember talking about my parents' vinyl record
of 1970s singer John Denver's *Greatest Hits* album in nurs-
ery school, much to the bewilderment of my classmates and

teachers, because even then I was obsessed with music—and often older music that my peers didn't care about.

Doctors diagnosed me as Autistic around then, though I later came to understand I was experiencing a "milder" form of it: Asperger's syndrome. Because it has come out that Hans Asperger was a Nazi, I use the term "Autistic" today because Autism is a spectrum, with many presentations besides the (by neurotypical standards) severe ones, on which I definitely belong.

Some of my issues include:

⇨   difficulty with social interactions and nonverbal communication;

⇨   difficulty with physical coordination;

⇨   being extremely literal and having trouble grasping metaphors and figures of speech;

⇨   having strong sensory sensitivity issues;

⇨   being generally hypersensitive to language, including to criticism;

⇨   having especially picky preferences for food, music, and the way that I would like the world to work;

⇨   and having trouble comprehending other points of view.

I have trouble interpreting body language, and for many years, I struggled to understand that people needed to take their turn speaking in a conversation. As examples of sensory sensitivity, I am strongly averse to the smell of eggs cooking and hypersensitive to touch—I'm warning you, don't ever try to tickle me.

My favorite illustration from childhood of me not "getting" a figure of speech was with Michael Jackson's "Beat It." When I heard that song, I thought, "Beat what?" I came to (potentially) overthink this after hearing it for years because I saw an interview with Jackson on MTV where he said that the song's message was "self-explanatory." Clearly it wasn't.

I also heard a deluge of negative comments growing up about seemingly everything I did. One of the ones that hurt the most was at an overnight arts camp when I was 11, and a kid I thought was a friend berated me for 30 minutes in front of peers about all kinds of things he didn't like about me.

Not knowing any better, I internalized much of this negative feedback, even though I knew he was misunderstanding me when he said, "You don't *feel* music. You just know music trivia." As someone who loves music as much as I do, I worried for years that this barrage of insults led to part of me dying that day; I had put myself out there, performing songs and trying to be accepted for being myself, and clearly I wasn't accepted. It felt for a while like I would never try expressing myself as much again, but thankfully I didn't let those doubts stop me.

As a child, I also struggled with my listening abilities; I tended to talk *at* people about things I was interested in without involving them in the conversation; I was most definitely self-centered. One of the biggest gifts I have today is that with time and a lot of work and practice, my self-centeredness has lessened as my concern for service to others has grown.

In fifth grade, I had my first episode of depression. I made comments in class about needing to see Jack Kevorkian, the infamous doctor associated with assisted suicides, because I wanted to die. I felt awful all the time, dealing with severe mood swings and crying at the slightest inconvenience, like when I realized that a mathematical trick I had discovered in first grade was common knowledge.

For a brief time, part of how I dealt with my depression was by bullying others. I remember being mean to another kid, taunting him about his Attention Deficit Disorder, not knowing that I myself struggled with similar attention issues. I walked away from him one day after saying something mean to him about his issues, strutting and gloating while he was crying behind me. I still regret some of the ways I was mean at that point in my life. Like many a bully, I was hurting others because I was hurt, and I'm sure that it was obvious to others that I was mean to try to fit in. Since that year, though, I've worked really hard to not treat people with that kind of cruelty.

In ninth grade, my parents forced me to see a psychiatrist. I was screaming that I didn't need the help as the doctor was coming to our house because I refused to go see him, but it turned out to be a blessing. He prescribed me medications that I figured would help make me get better. I took very seriously the daily regimen of taking my meds, and I still do because I do not ever want to regress to be that violent little kid again. My meds are the primary reason I've never touched alcohol or drugs as an adult because I can't risk going back to where I was. Ever.

In high school, I came out of the metaphorical closet, though everyone knew I was gay anyway. That provided another layer of complications to what I was already going through. When I was a freshman, I told the most popular guy in school I liked him and got a lot of shit for being a "faggot." As I grew into myself and realized that I fit fewer stereotypes than I thought, I would try to fit in by acting like a stereotypically flamboyant gay guy. I remember saying things like, "Go, girl!" to people in theatre productions that I was a part of when I was a senior. That got me the label of "poser gay" by a couple of straight kids who clearly understood nothing about me. They weren't alone.

One person with whom I didn't get along in high school and who has since become a friend has said to me, "You were misunderstood. People didn't know what to do with you." I didn't fit in any kind of metaphorical box that was legible to others, including the school administration. Years later, I started getting messages on social media from bullies apologizing for what they did to me back in high school. They didn't know how it had affected others in terms of eating disorders or anything else, but they were right to realize that how they treated me was not okay.

I got into a small liberal arts college that I started immediately after high school. Even if I wasn't academically ready to manage my own time, I needed to get the fuck out of my hometown. I came out as gay the first week I was there to a crowd full of strangers and was largely accepted with open arms. I met real, close friends for the first time, including other music nerds who had felt misunderstood, too. I made a conscious effort to treat others differently than how I had been treated, and I became friends with everyone from local coffeeshop workers to students from different backgrounds from all over the world.

Still, being in the middle of the American Midwest during winters and other times could prove mighty depressing, especially because I abstained from alcohol and drugs and often felt left out. During my second year, I started noticing how happy people were when I went to parties, because they knew I found the drinking and drugging atmosphere to be toxic. Despite being welcomed in social settings, I still felt alone. In January of 2009, in the middle of my third year, I strongly considered overdosing on pills; ended up reaching out to the wrong people, including a professor; and almost got kicked out of school for being openly suicidal. Those pills could have led to the ultimate silence for me.

It seems to me that creativity, artistic or otherwise, is the opposite of silence because it involves expressing myself, even if it's just to me. For the majority of my life to date, I didn't feel like I was creative. When I was growing up, I longed to express myself in ways that would make others listen and rethink how they were treating me. I have a feeling that finding my creative voice wouldn't have changed anything external, but it still would have helped me. In tenth grade, I won a small talent contest for my singing the Smashing Pumpkins' 1990s alternative rock classic, "Today," a cappella. Singing by myself brought me and others joy, and I had always listened to lots of music in headphones. I thought about creating original music, but it seemed like more of an ordeal because I just wasn't inspired.

During that time, I was also trying to discover my voice as a writer, academically and otherwise. I always had a flair for words, going at least back to middle school, when an English teacher wrote in my report card, "I can't wait to see Josh's work published in the not too distant future!" In high school, though, I completed a three-week school project with Greg Kot, the rock critic from the *Chicago Tribune*, studying heavy metal and hip hop. Those weeks were probably the highlight of my childhood, but my academic writing skills were solid but still somewhat lacking in high school.

But my freshman year of college had at least two milestone events that helped me discover my creativity through writing and music. These events forever altered my ideas about my creativity: I took two freshman writing seminars with an incredible but tough English professor named Anupama Arora who taught me how to write for academic audiences; and I wrote my first full song that I was ever proud of.

It had taken a long road to get there, but I'm so grateful that I discovered my creativity at all. In kindergarten, I tried making up a story and ended up plagiarizing one about dinosaurs from an audiocassette that I had absorbed. I couldn't come up with a story of my own—yet. I could never come up with ideas for Halloween costumes; I still can't. In second grade, I tried trick-or-treating dressed up as Paul Simon with an inflatable guitar—that's about as creative as I got with Halloween. So, for most of my life, I had thought I wasn't creative, or at least that I was "creativity challenged."

Growing up, I knew I was mentally different, and with my form of Autism, I didn't have much of an imagination for fictional stories. But I could memorize song lyrics, lists of the U.S. presidents, people's birthdays, and long monologues. My way of thinking, by definition, was creative and unique, but that doesn't mean that I thought I could create much of anything in terms of art.

My brother was invested in drawing and painting, so I initially understood creativity to mean *visual* creativity. To this day, I see a beautiful painting and have no idea how to analyze it like a visual artist would. My Autism, by neurotypical standards, skews how my brain organizes visual information, so I notice different things in visual art that most people do, like when I experience a disparate series of dots with pretty colors.

I always "got" music, though. More than most people, I felt certain sounds down to my bones. To this day, pianos and acoustic guitars, beautiful melodies, and gorgeous vocal harmonies penetrate my soul like nothing else. I still struggle to find words to describe music's sound, but there's no question that music matters more to me than just about anything else in my life.

My brain also absorbs names and dates like a sponge; I can name a musical event for every year for over 100 consecutive years. I never liked huge concerts, though— between the social anxiety and the sensory overload with noise and lights, they've never been much fun, but give me a recording I love in headphones, and I'm happy all day.

In my earliest years, I wanted to be a musician, but I had trouble writing songs of my own, and a lot of it had to do with a lack of confidence or inspiration. I also got a lot of crap in high school for my singing in choir and drama productions and for my writing in English classes. So, not having any way of knowing better, I internalized a lot of the dominant neurotypical culture's ideas of what was and wasn't "good" art, singing, writing, and creativity.

And just like in kindergarten, I still have trouble writing fictional stories and songs, but I've grown to be able to incorporate my life into creative nonfiction and songwriting based on my experiences. This led to a shift in college, both in terms of my creativity and social acceptance, which helped lift me out of a suicidal depression. However, what led to my creative breakthrough was not my newly-found acceptance, but the painful lack of acceptance I had experienced until then. I had no idea that what this breakthrough yielded would bring me more joy and acceptance than I had ever dreamed was possible for me.

During high school, I tried writing songs with a few guitar chords, but I hated my lyrics. They didn't sound good; they didn't sound like me. They felt forced, like when someone tries to do something because they feel they should be able to do it well but can't. I tried everything, albeit infrequently. And then in 2006, during my freshman year of college, I got inspired with a long list of insults and a little tune.

I had become friends with an older student who, at the time, really didn't "get" me. They may have liked me and found me amusing in some ways, but when it came to my Autism, they sounded to me—and to others—like they blamed me for their issues with my disabilities. For example, they made harsh comments about their frustration with how literal I am and other issues that I couldn't (and still can't) control, and when they were kind, it felt condescending; it was more like, "Awww, you're so cute, you actually mean what you say because you're so literal." I must admit, though, that I was extremely needy at the time, and I didn't understand social boundaries, so that didn't help this person's already high stress level working on their various commitments as a student and otherwise. But whether or not my feelings were justified, I was pissed about how they were acting towards me.

One day, I was walking around campus and I had many of their—and others'—insults swirling around in my head, and suddenly, like divine inspiration, I started to hum a repetitive tune and rhythm, and I realized, "This could be a song. I need to write this down."

So, I went to my smelly dorm room—I was struggling with basic hygiene at the time—and wrote down this list of insults, some that others had overtly said to me and others that had been implied. For example, no one had ever said explicitly that I stared at them too long, but they'd sure acted like it. The inspiration that had been lacking for so long suddenly poured out of me, and within an hour, I had a song about my Autism.

That was the first song I'd ever written that made me feel proud. It is still my favorite of my original songs because of how much it has positively affected other people, too. Writing this song led me to experience a turning point in my life around the same time I wanted to die during my third year of college. My seemingly nonexistent creativity thus caused one of my life's greatest triumphs.

A few hours after I wrote that song as a freshman, I performed it for three friends in one of their dorm rooms.

I knew it was special to me, but after that I stashed it away for two years because I thought nobody would like it; it was too self-centered, I reasoned. Then, at a college house open mic in the fall of 2008, in addition to singing and playing customary folky covers of others' material, I played this song and was shocked when it got more applause than anything I'd done in my entire life. People were laughing at certain lines, including side comments that I made after some, and cheering at others. By the end, a couple dozen people were cheering loudly, and suddenly, I realized I had something to say that a lot of people needed to hear.

A couple months later, I auditioned for a benefit concert for a few members of its steering committee, and they loved my original song—way more, in fact, than they loved the covers where I thought my voice sounded far better. There was something unique about this song, and around two months later, before the concert, I heard that people had been buzzing around campus that I was going to do something spectacular at this concert.

That night, when I got on stage, I could hear people cheering for me, and I said, "Okay, so, two things. The first thing is, this is a song—a song that I wrote—and the thing about this song is, this is a song that is unequivocally about *me*, and the second thing is, when I say, 'I was never wrong,' I don't mean about facts; I mean about my existence."

The audience, many of whom came to hear the popular main a cappella group on campus, likely didn't know what to expect when I started furiously playing basic chords and singing this list of insults, pretty much exactly like this:

Some people say I smell, some people say I stare at them too long
Some people say I withdraw too much, but I can't help that
Some people say my brain is wired so I have trouble making
friends easily
Some people say I cling like an anchor sinks ships to whomever
reaches out to me

But I know what I am, and I can tell you now
That I have come so far and that I can show you how
I can be a person with far less self-consciousness around you
And I will be anything, because I reach out

Some people say I take things far too literally and personally
Some people say I use too many, like, extra-grammatical phrases, like
Some people say I'm too sensitive to ever take criticism well, like
Some people say I'm also too critical to ever sit back and enjoy life
Some people say I give too much thought to every little detail, like
Some people say I don't find room for anything important
Some people say I yell right in their ears . . . yeah
Like some people said that they knew I was gay for years!

But I know that I can learn as well as anyone, and
I know that I have enough courage to stand up
For others when they really need it so that I can be an asset
So please don't misunderstand if I just don't get something you say

I am kind and I am sweet and I am smart and I am a good person
I am something more than what you might expect from me
I may mess things up from time to time, but I will never hurt you
Unless you hurt me first, so please don't ever hurt me first

Some people say I don't get subtleties unless they hit me over the head
Some people say that I hold grudges for too long
Some people say that my world's limits are choices and self-
imposed, but

61

Some such people just don't know, no, no

'Cause I know what I am, despite if you tell me otherwise
And I'll keep doing what I do, even if it means that I can't compromise
I can't be what isn't me, so please don't ever try to make me change
And I will be anything because I was never wrong

And then I finished off the song with a bit para-phrased from a certain song by the Police from 1983:

Every breath I take, every move I make
Every smile I don't fake, I was never wrong
Every single day, every word I say
Every game I don't play, I was never
Wrong.

While I was singing, the crowd cheered when I said the line about being gay. When I sang the line about having trouble making friends, I heard, "Awww." And they clapped when I sang about how I don't hurt people unless they hurt me first. And as I finished the song, the place *exploded.*

As I started to walk off the stage, I felt stunned because my song about my Autism was getting all these people to stand up and cheer, when I had always assumed that no one would find it special the way I did.

This was the first time I performed an original song for a big audience, and I felt beyond affirmed. I knew that I was loved, funny, honest, brave . . . and finally, accepted. My dream of others' acceptance, on my terms, had come true. In the span of maybe three minutes, I went from tak-ing my courage for granted to having a group of people affirm how amazing and brave I was.

During the intermission afterwards, many people came up to me to tell me how they wanted a copy of my song recorded, how they could relate to certain parts of it, and how they had been in tears. I get emotional today just thinking about it. All these people who came to hear that heavily hyped a cappella group had stood up and cheered for *my* song, and in droves.

Two days later, my music professor, a classical musicologist, asked to shake my hand, telling me how much he appreciated my performance. One friend told me later, "Josh, that is the only thing that people will remember from that concert!" Others have told me that my song is universal; I never saw that compliment coming in a million years.

About two weeks later, my former academic advisor saw me in a bakery in town and said, "You know, the song is called 'Some People Say,' but what about the things I said?" He meant, what about the compliments he and others had given me? So that summer, I started to write a new ending for my song, which I've amended since. Here is the ending of the song that I perform now instead of the "Every Breath You Take" rewrite:

Some people say I'm gonna make a mark on this world
Some people tell me I'm a star and a genius
Some people say there needs to be more people in this world like me

Some people say that I contribute lots to my community
Some people say that I inspire them and write so beautifully
Some people say that my existence isn't a mistake and their hero is me

Some people say the difference that I make is really obvious
Some people say that others' insults of me were just ignorant

Some people say that my singing and songwriting are gifts and I
should always be proud of me

Some people say that I deserved a standing ovation
For everything I do at my college graduation
Some people say that I rock this earth and they love me and
they'll never forget me, yeah

And I know what I am, even though I did not for so long
And I know that I can do good because I've already
Accomplished so much more than for what I once gave myself
credit
And though some might still put me down, I'll do what I can to
not let it get to me
'Cause I am smart, and yes, I am beautiful, sometimes straightforward
and at others inscrutable
But no matter what some people say, I know that I am here to stay!

When I first wrote the original version of the song,
I didn't believe in myself. For a long time, I had to act my
way into really believing that I was worthy of what I was
saying about myself in contrast to all the insults. But the
more I performed the song, the more I started to believe
it. Although it shouldn't have taken others' validation to
convince me to believe in myself, I'm grateful for all of
the validation I received, even if my process of believing
in myself has never been perfect. Especially in the last few
years, I have believed in myself like never before.

At the time, I also took for granted how courageous
it was for me to write a song like this and play it for others. But like Bob Dylan wrote in "Tangled Up in Blue,"
"Every one of them words rang true and glowed like

burning coal, pouring off of every page like it was written in my soul from me to you."

My song, "Some People Say," was written in my soul—inscribed, etched, burned—from me to you—to anyone who hears it or reads the lyrics. It wasn't just for me after all.

Since then, I've occasionally performed the song in other places. One of the most moving contexts in which I performed it was at a summer camp where I volunteered as a counselor. It's a camp for children with Autism and/or Tourette's syndrome. I sang my favorite original song for a group of kids who understood exactly what I was talking about.

Though "Some People Say" was originally written as a way to cope with a friend being hurtful and oppressive about my Autism, there's a lot of humor in the song, too, and ultimately, it's triumphant. Its basic message is that some people say all this stuff about me, but I know that I'm better than that. And all these camp kids heard my words and got what I was trying to convey. I've rarely had such a moving an experience playing for anyone.

I also performed the song at an open mic for singer-songwriters at the Old Town School of Folk Music in Chicago, and one of the professional musicians and teachers there said, "I wish I could write a song as direct as yours."

More recently, when I performed it as part of the tenth anniversary of a concert series called Acoustic Explosion in Chicago, the next act said, "I can't follow that. That was amazing." This song still gives me chills and makes me—and others—feel something every time I perform it.

My life was never the same after that concert performance during college in 2009. As before, I put a lot of work into making deep friendships on campus and into getting involved—including singing, songwriting, newspaper editing, work at the radio station, and work with different social justice organizations. But I had no clue how appreciated I was until May 8, 2010, when hundreds of people gave me a standing ovation when I walked at my college's 2010 graduation ceremony. I was told that when people started standing up for me, I stopped "like a deer in headlights" and then smiled like no one had ever seen me smile. Like that standing ovation when I first performed "Some People Say," I never saw this coming either. Many people came up to me that day telling me how much of a difference I had made on that campus.

Despite these victories, a year after I walked at that graduation ceremony, I found myself at my most miserable while I was living at home. I came back to that campus for another graduation and, haunted by memories at home of years of bullying, I almost drank alcohol with pills and then, after I couldn't open the bottle of alcohol, I intentionally ran across a road with no stoplight, not caring if I lived or died. I almost got hit by a car.

Two nights later, a friend who I had only had one serious conversation with up to that point saw me walking down the street and offered to take a walk with me. I doubt he knew just how awful I had been feeling, but as we started to walk down the street—the same street I had walked down for years feeling lonely because I wasn't going to all the college parties going on, he was going out of his way to let me know how loved and appreciated I was, that I was beautiful, and that I had deserved that standing ovation a year before. I felt like I belonged and was deeply understood, and I believe he saved my life. This is someone for whom I had expressed strong feelings, saying that he was beautiful and that I felt ugly when I saw him. I never expected a straight crush of mine to care like that about me. I was stunned when he did that.

This story proves that even after moments of triumph, I can still struggle—and that's okay. Mental health struggles in my life haven't gone away, but with outside help, including community and medications, they have gotten much, much better.

Since then, so much has changed. I moved into Chicago from my hometown in the suburbs, got into graduate school after three years of trying, have had many articles published, presented at multiple conferences, won multiple awards, and joined an international English honor society—quite a feat given my trouble with metaphors and figurative language. And recently, I started teaching a dream-come-true course on contemporary writing about music at the university where I got my master's degree.

I don't perform music often, but I recently gave my first paid lecture about music and Autism and got to play a couple of my songs as part of it. The audience told me how much they were inspired by and appreciated my music and my story. The weird thing is that today, many people don't "get" that I'm Autistic, or even that I'm that different from others, but when I tell my story, people listen and appreciate where I'm coming from with my struggles.

If I "don't seem Autistic/disabled" to some, I don't take that as progress; it's just part of my journey. I still struggle with being hyper-literal, with major social anxiety in new situations, and with sensory sensitivity issues. I also have yet to meet anyone close to "Mr. Right," but I have faith that he will present himself if and when the time comes.

And speaking of faith, a big part of my life that's helped me get out of my own way is spirituality. I don't believe in the God of the Bible, but I believe there's something out there greater than me that helps me get through my day. I call that force God, but it took me years to even conceive of such a force.

Since I started cultivating my spirituality, including connecting it to my creativity, a lot of things have gotten easier. Today my mother and I have a great relationship, and I work hard to listen to her and others in a way that I could not dream of when I was a kid. A lot of that comes with continued practice in social situations, ones I still tend to overthink and analyze to death before and after they happen. The good news is that I'm getting better at staying present and not trying to control everything, at least in the moment when social situations happen.

So, what works for me today includes: medications, music, creativity, community, and spirituality, as well as abstinence from alcohol and drugs. All of these, in different ways, have shown up in my life when I have taken the action to find and use them. In that moment when I sang my song and spoke my truth, my life changed because all of those factors, including spirituality—my Higher Power was looking out for me to be in the right place at the right time so that my message could be received.

To be clear, I don't believe everything in the world happens for a good and godly reason. Some things occur because of injustice, including ableism and heterosexism/homophobia. But I'm learning to even be grateful for what I went through growing up; it made me stronger and more prepared to deal with the world. Don't get me wrong, I still struggle with anger and resentment, so nothing is perfect, but I am so much further along in many areas of my life than I used to be.

Today, I have an advanced degree in a field in which I have struggled: English, specifically literature. I have used my degrees to get more work in what I am good at, which has now led to five years of professional writing tutoring— not bad for someone who was called "retarded" for their writing in high school.

Getting into graduate school was one of several turning points in my life, but the biggest breakthrough I've ever had was becoming aware that I am creative when I wrote "Some People Say." While I was processing some serious vitriol from others and myself, my ostensibly absent creativity changed my life. And performing it and gaining a community of people telling me how much they could relate to it? That was one of my life's most stunning surprises.

Some things will never change. I still listen to a lot of the same songs I've been listening to for years, even decades. And I'm still literal as all hell, as the metaphorical expression would have it, and I still struggle with new social situations. But the message I want to convey is that there is always hope. I can't promise things will always get better, as I've had a lot of both good luck and resources as well as a lot of perseverance to help me get through hard times.

But today, I accept my Autism as a kind of super-power, in part because I have a memory like no one else's. As I wrote earlier, I can name a musical event from every year from today going back over a century. 1909? Jazz clarinetist Benny Goodman was born. 2019? Lady Gaga won an Oscar for cowriting the song, "Shallow" from *A Star is Born*. That doesn't mean that I have gratitude for every circumstance in my life, but I'm getting closer to there.

I might seem well-adjusted now, but it's taken a lot of time and action to get up to this point. Today, people sometimes tell me that they hear parallels between where I was and where they are now, and between where I am now and where they want to be. That inspires *me* to keep going. And to paraphrase Ralph Waldo Emerson, if one *other* life breathes easier because of what I do, I have succeeded.

Now, that's a life I'm proud to have led. And the best part? I don't have to be silent anymore. One of my most cherished sayings come from Paul Simon, the singer-songwriter I grew up listening to more than any other: "The fighter still remains." It surprises me that I often think of a metaphor to sum up my life, but I have the heart of a fighter because of everything I've been through and the strength I've developed.

I don't fight in isolation. I know I am not alone. And as Elton John famously sang, "I'm still standing better than I ever did, lookin' like a true survivor, feelin' like a little kid."

Except, in the interest of overthinking this, like I often do, I will say that I feel better than I ever did as a little kid. So, technically I'm feeling like an adult. What a miracle.

And to quote one more song that my mom used to call my theme song: "Joshua fought the battle of Jericho and the walls came tumbling down."

I would be remiss if I didn't mention another song that I wrote for myself. It was untitled until a friend, Alec Henriksen, killed himself, so this is for anyone who's struggling who could use some hope:

"Alec's Song"

It took a long time to realize I am someone
Let alone to translate it into words
When the whole world seems to tell you that you're wrong
You grow up thinking your life is absurd
Well, trust me, even if you've never been able to trust anyone
The best friend you'll ever have is time
As long as you aren't too hard on yourself
You will move forward whether or not you try

Chorus: *You are not alone, and I have hope for you*
You are worth more than you might think now
Affirm your dignity, go out there, and keep doing what you do
And I know one day you will be proud

Struggle can lead to feeling worn down and tired
Make you feel like you're worth nothin' at all
But I'll be damned if your life is worthless
Know that you never need to crawl
All those bullies I dealt with when I was younger
I know now that they were wrong
And anyone who puts you down is no better
Than you could ever be all along

Chorus

*You are not ugly, you are not hopeless, and you are better than
you are thinking
You don't need to take refuge in distractions like drinking
You are beautiful, you are right, and you have life on your side
So, keep being you and say out loud with pride:
I am (I am) somebody (somebody)
I am (I am) somebody (somebody)
I am (I am) somebody (somebody)
I am (I am) somebody (somebody)*

Chorus 2x

*And I know one day you will be proud to say:
I am somebody.*

May the same come true for you. May you always know that you are not alone.

Acknowledgments: part of this chapter has some content taken from this original story that I had previously published, "6 Moments When Music Made My Life Better," at the Good Men Project website: https://goodmenproject.com/featured-content/6-moments-when-music-made-my-life-better-bbab/. Permission given by the piece's editor, Barbara Abramson.

Also, "Some People Say" and "Alec's Song" are copyright 2019 by Joshua Daniel Friedberg. Used by permission.

MY WILD, BEAUTIFUL LIFE: FROM DARKNESS AND DESOLATION TO LOVING THE SKIN I'M IN

By: Julie Raborn

The loud buzzing of blended voices in the bar went silent to my ears. The dim lights that engulfed me faded to darkness, and my eyesight blurred from the shock of the sharp words I'd just heard. I felt as heavy as cement and couldn't catch my breath.

It was a lovely, crisp fall night downtown with friends. We were having a few drinks and great laughter, enjoying life together. I noticed after a while that one of my friends had become sullen and was struggling to tell me something. They were withdrawn from conversation, being abnormally quiet, and had a sad look on their face. Unable to withhold this painful secret any longer, they confessed it to me. They couldn't bear any longer knowing all that

I was oblivious to, and they were angry and hurt it was happening. I leaned in gently and asked, "Are you all right? What is wrong? Please tell me because I know something is really wrong." He shook his head and kept staring down into his near-empty beer. I could see he was torn up over the situation and was struggling to say the words. Trying to lighten the mood I jokingly asked, "What, is it Jake?" He lifted his head and looked me directly in the eye not saying a word. "What, is Jake cheating on me?" and I start laughing because that was a ridiculous impossibility but what I used to tease about in the moment. He nodded and kept eye contact with me, making it very clear he was not joking.

"What the fuck is going on, what are you talking about?" He slowly responded, "Yes, Jake is cheating on you. I am so disgusted by him doing this to you and couldn't hold this from you any longer."

Trying to wrap my head around this, I ask, "How long has this been going on and who is she?"

He tells me, "It's been months, and she works near the area that he does. It makes me sick when he tells me how they sex text all the time when they're apart."

In this moment I was informed that the man I planned to marry had been cheating on me. For months. He provided other details about their affair that devastated me. I had no clue and never would have thought this man would cheat on me. I fully believed in and trusted our love and commitment.

Anger and disbelief brought me to my feet and out the door into the starry night. I aimlessly walked in heels along the lonely city streets as traffic roared past, rattling my desperation for silence and relief. I was painfully experiencing the validation, yet again, that I am not good enough and would never be truly loved.

As a little girl, too young a girl, I experienced emotions and beliefs that I couldn't handle. I couldn't tolerate the depth and greatness of them, and this shaped my identity. They became the roots of the issues I still battle to this day. Sometimes I have beautiful victories over them and sometimes I have sloppy, painful losses. Through mindset work and conscious, soul-aligned living instead of numbed-out, dysfunctional autopilot, I am now capable of actually *feeling* them instead of resisting them. I have embraced my authentic self by taking action on my desires and what I want to feel by creating my experiences through my thoughts and actions. These have been courageous steps out of pain and darkness and into healing.

I now always take essential time for myself to reflect on and heal from the painful experiences I have had in my life when thoughts surface in my mind and emotions swirl inside from them. On a cool fall evening, I had been deeply exploring my thoughts and emotions through journaling. My blush-colored Himalayan pashmina was draped around me as I sat, curled up on the couch in silence, staring at the flickering flame of the candle on my coffee table. From the open window a crisp breeze danced across my cheek, clarity shining down on the deep thoughts in the darkest corners of my mind. The most deep-rooted fears I've uncovered along my awakening journey are that I'm not good enough and will never be truly loved. Like a fast-spinning movie reel, I had flashes of endless moments in my life that had taken hold when I was that unaware little girl and on through the years. Now, I was realizing that these experiences running through my mind had reinforced these core beliefs all along. Cupping my warm mug of tea, I became conscious of what have been my most painful, damaging feelings that have caused so much suffering. I have always wanted nothing more than to be loved for who I am without pressure or expectations from others to change, to feel safe, and to belong. But these things have always felt threatened and scarce.

Growing up, my mother made delicious, hearty meals and large portions for a family of six. The savory smell of roast in the oven, chili made from scratch or an apple pie would fill the house and tease my taste buds in anticipation. That is what I was used to; I never knew any differently. It was comforting to overeat this delicious food. It made me feel so loved being cared for by my mother (who is the greatest, most lovely gift from God), and enjoying a beautifully set dinner table with silverware properly placed.

I didn't recognize it as overeating until about age 9 or 10, when I realized I was the "chubby girl" compared to my friends. If I sat on my dad's lap he would say, "Honey you're like a bag of bricks." Or, "You're crushing my legs, sweetie." He wasn't aware of the impact of his teasing words, despite how much he loved me. Around 11 years-old, I started idolizing women of beauty and glamour like Madonna, Cindy Crawford, models in magazines—thin and gorgeous, and actresses in movies and on TV. I wanted so much to be like all of these women; they were so beautiful and desired. I thought wow, that's the life, and it's where all the love and happiness are. At about age 15, I came to understand that I was emotionally eating for comfort in the face of the hardships I was facing from bullies, societal pressures, and battling my own shame.

I started noticing how thin my friends were compared to me, especially in my uniforms for basketball and cheerleading and because I couldn't fit into most junior girl clothing at the department stores. During my childhood, no one had ingrained in me a fitness and health focused routine. I didn't know any differently. I thought we were a pretty normal family, but as I started growing up and seeing how many other kids were doing activities with their families, I noticed the differences. I made it mean bad things about myself, such as, I am not special or good enough to have those experiences; I didn't have a strong enough sense of self to rationalize it.

If you grew up in the 80's with curves, you know that clothes were made stick straight and gave no mercy for any curviness. Begrudgingly I'd walk through the junior girls clothing sections in stores, hearing gossip and fast chatter from women around me while I browsed rack after rack with lackluster. It was aggravating to try on the cute, trendy clothes in the messy dressing rooms with the unflattering fluorescent lighting, wanting them to fit so badly, like the coveted Guess jeans. I would stare at my thighs and hips through the reflection in the mirror, feeling tears well up in my eyes. I heard the voices of others in changing rooms having random conversations, but louder than that, I heard my own sighs of disappointment and nasty comments about myself rumbling through my head. "You're so ugly and fat," and "Why do you even try because you don't even matter," played on repeat in my head. Not only could I not fit into them well after tugging and pulling, but the high-priced name brands weren't a priority. The real priorities for our family were normal living costs, food and taking care of our basic needs, not the faded, button-fly Guess jeans that I thought would make me someone special and beautiful.

I always found it scary to trust girls, mostly because I received the rotten mean-girl treatment. I was snickered at and bullied about my looks, my body, and my clothes. One day, I walked into English class having tried out a new cozy look with black workout leggings and a roomy red t-shirt.

A few girls huddled together and laughed while look-ing at me and saying, "What in the hell is she wearing?! She looks so stupid!" I put my head down and stared at the drab tile flooring as I found my way to my desk. I sunk into the hard, wooden seat feeling warm tears well up and my cheeks flushed with embarrassment. Trying to figure out who I was and where I belonged among many dif-ferent cliques in school produced so much loneliness and nasty judgments; nasty judgments from others and my own self-judgment. I've always felt like I was on the out-side looking in. Self-depreciating humor and binge eating helped numb out these discomforts. Despite the treatment I received from other teenagers, it seemed to me that we were all just trying to find our way in the world, while deep down we were scared and uncertain.

I'll never forget the cold winter day when I was walking home from school at about 11-years-old when two neighbor-hood girls who often bullied me got physical. Thick snow was falling fast as I walked the mile home along a well beaten path

I remember well to this day. Taunting me from behind, I heard them yell, "You're so fat and ugly! You're such a loser!" They were suddenly right behind me and pushed me down hard to the ground into the snow. I was in shock as they pushed and kicked me, continuing the hurtful and nasty remarks. "You're a nobody! You're such a joke!" In a daze and sore from the beating, I found my way to my feet and ran home, crying the entire way. I went straight upstairs to my bed, curling up in my quilt that felt like my security blanket.

The bullying didn't stop when I grew up, it just came in different forms from adults who acted like nasty children. I experienced it in the workplace and even in friendships and intimate relationships.

I will never forget the nightmare roller coaster rides of emotions, heartbreak and deep pain I felt when I found out the love of my life and soon to be fiancé had been cheating on me; my dreams of marriage and children with him were shattered.

I will never forget a boyfriend that yelled out to me from a backyard party with a couple dozen people looking on as I drove away after collecting a couple of my things from him, "Why don't you lose some weight bitch, you might look better!"

I will never forget trying multiple times to get out of a relationship with a physically abusive boyfriend and the time it finally was successful was a night he held a gun to my head with his other arm choking me around my neck... and how beyond thankful I am that I survived this and he finally got out of my life for good.

I will never forget when a boyfriend became distant and cold, and started acting strange and alienating me after several months of being together. Come to find he didn't want to be with me because I was curvy and he prefers very thin women.

I will never forget when I was beaten to the point of having a concussion, bruised knuckles and broken nails trying to protect myself. The police showed up at my door knowing, without question, I had been beaten by my boyfriend. I said everything was fine and that I would be ok because I was absolutely terrified of any consequences in my life from him, or his family and friends, if they hauled him off to jail. I'll never forget the concern and anger in both of those officer's eyes over what had happened to me.

It took me until my mid-30's to realize that hurt people hurt people. I now know that it's the solution they come up with to avoid feeling their own pain and fears. Bullies choose to take out their struggles on others, which only perpetuates their issues and keeps them acting out in fear and judgment. Lashing out at others is a way to avoid our own bullshit and feel a sense of authority and control in doing so.

When I was 15, I lived out of state with my mother for a few months, not too long after my parents divorced. It was an affluent area that was very different from where I grew up. I did not "show like money" like many others in the school and in my neighborhood. I was not sporting Abercrombie and Fitch, or short shorts paired with plaid knee-high socks and wooden clogs. I rode the bus to high school for the few months I went there.

"Hi, I'm Julie, I think you live right near me," I said on one of my first bus rides to a girl that lived up the street. Her face scowled in judgment as she gave me the once-over look, rolled her eyes and walked away to sit with her friends. I slumped into the hard seat and stared out the window feeling flushed with rejection and shame holding my pink backpack tight. Similar events happened in the hallways at school. Eventually I gave up trying. I felt shunned, as if I was in some sort of movie where I was the poor girl going to the rich kid school and was rejected, ignored, and never spoken to. This was except for one girl, a pure gift from God, and one of my best friends to this day. I truly have no idea what I would do without her in my life.

When I was about 16, I realized that my emotional eating was a problem. I wanted food even when I wasn't actually hungry to comfort myself and fill the voids inside. I was envious of other girls who were thin, athletic and seemingly winning in life compared to me. I made our differences mean something bad and wrong about me, instead of us simply being different as we are uniquely intended to be. Over the years I tried out diets and sporadic, hardcore bursts of exercise, while continuing to binge eat to not feel my emotions and to self-medicate. I paid for a gym membership for a few years that I rarely used and eventually stopped using altogether. I couldn't bring myself to walk into the gym with how much shame I had about myself and thinking everyone was looking at me and judging me.

Food was like a drug that numbed my sadness and loneliness. I was trying to protect myself from not being hurt by anyone, men or women. It wasn't an intentional or conscious process. I discovered later that on a subconscious level, I was choosing to engage in this destructive behavior to protect myself from being abused, but this behavior was self-afflicted abuse. I wasn't protecting myself *from* myself or nourishing my body how I truly needed. I was unknowingly and unintentionally living with a victim mentality. I was unaware of this distorted identity I'd created that was exponentially destructive mentally, emotionally and physically.

Despite how poorly so many girls treated me, I still wanted to belong with them, to be popular, thin, a striking beauty, have the money and seemingly carefree life, as well as family vacations like they did. Surprisingly, over the years I became friends here and there with the bullies, but it never really felt genuine and safe. I felt like some sort of outsider or outcast; I didn't feel I genuinely belonged anywhere.

My lack of belonging compounded with the pressure I received from men, society at large, and other women, who acted like fiercely competitive clawing wildcats. My perception was that I had to be thin and hot or I wouldn't be worthy, wanted, or lovable. Sometimes I would encounter evidence in my life that supported these beliefs, such as when I discovered that night that my almost-fiancé had been cheating on me. Many boyfriends said painful and cruel things to me about my looks and body. They said things like I should look like the girls on magazine covers or like one of my closest friends, who happened to be thin and blonde.

One hot summer day, at almost 18-years-old, my boyfriend and I pulled into the gas station to fill up his red Mustang.

I walked to go inside and get a cold drink as he barked at me, "Why don't you have an ass on you like her?" In astonishment I turned to see who he was referring to. It was that closest thin, blonde friend of mine pumping gas at another pump. "Fuck you" was my immediate and only response in that brutal moment etched in my memory.

All of this made me believe I was fat, ugly, not good, pretty, or special enough, and that I didn't matter or belong. I felt lost and didn't have a solid sense of belonging at home or at school, or within myself. What I didn't realize until years later was that the core of what I sincerely wanted was to be loved and accepted just as I was. I now know and understand why I was desperately seeking approval and self-worth from anywhere but within myself. Somehow that seemed more valuable and important than actually loving myself as I am, or even loving myself at all. I did not feel I had any worth or that I would ever be loved or seen as the beautiful woman I dreamed of being. I could never be that striking beauty; I would never be good enough. I was the invisible, chubby brunette friend. I learned that if you're seeking validation externally, you'll always be seeking, because the only true fulfillment is from within. I eventually realized I simply had an hourglass figure, which is beautiful and coveted. I didn't view myself this way until many years later, and even then, I still struggled to believe I was enough.

By the time I reached my thirties, I knew I wanted so much more in life, though I didn't quite know how to have or be more, or that I was even worthy or good enough for more. For years on end, I was in a lonely and depressive state that kept worsening this "not enoughness" that impacted many different areas of my life. I was suffering and noticed how often I cried and felt in a fog. I felt like I was dragging heavy chains I couldn't free myself from and was so deprived of joy in my life.

Unease tingled through me every day as I felt the discomfort of my body from the weight gain over the years. My shirt felt too clingy to my stomach and hips, and my pants too snug all over. I pulled on my shirt as if adjusting it would change the way it will look or feel, though it didn't; I somehow convinced myself it would. I thought, maybe if I suck in my stomach? But I couldn't keep holding in my stomach.

I would catch a glimpse of my reflection in the mirror and barely made eye contact with myself. I was somehow staying stuck in the part of my mind that was comfortably rich with denial, while talking myself into believing I looked partly cute in the outfit to somehow force myself out into the world. The sound of my own voice uttering negative digs from disappointment and disgust of my too-curvy shape looped loudly in my mind as I observed how uncomfortable I really was. "You are such a fatass and look horrible." "You are so pathetic for not losing this damn weight already." "No one will ever love you looking like this." "Gross, you are so fucking fat."

The shrill alarm would jar me awake each morning not long after finally having fallen into a deep sleep. I forced my body out of bed in mere survival mode to keep a roof over my head and faced the dreaded stress at work. Thoughts started spinning on the daily repeat reel of problems, to-do's and the constant random and dramatic mind chatter. After a hot shower and my first few sips of coffee with organic cream during my morning routine, hearing "Today is going to be hell and you've got to just push through" looping in my mind, I pulled on my "mask." Its heaviness laden with insecurity, shame and fear weighed on my entire body. My flirty, fun-loving side that said, "Things are going pretty damn well in my life and I'm feeling awesome!" is what others perceived when I was hiding behind this mask so I could hide from my dark shadow places. I put it on to attempt not to feel other's judgments and opinions of me, as well as not feel my own, try to fake out stress and discomfort, and conceal what I'm truly feeling.

Call after call obnoxiously beeped through my headset as I tried to maintain my kind nature amidst consistent upsets and demands from people. "I hate this job, I hate my life, and I can't take this anymore," was on constant replay in my mind. I had been on auto-pilot going through the motions each day. Drained after another long call by a client who had taken their frustration out on me for some error the company caused or some unmet expectation, I placed my head in my hands for a few moments before documenting the call and taking yet another. I briefly glanced out the window, watching the leaves rustle in the wind. I felt that anxious urgency through my body to get to the next call because of the busy nature of the call center. I was mentally exhausted from years of this consistent stress and the irrational expectations to have a 99.97% performance rate and cringed every time the email arrived in my inbox showing my monthly performance. I felt stuck by pressure and the need for money and insurance benefits instead of having happiness and job contentment in my life.

The stress and unhappiness at work, along with emotional binge eating, weight struggles, and self-destructive behaviors, had become a daily battle. These threads perpetuated and fed off each other. I felt swallowed whole by it all. I constantly glanced at the time on my computer, counting down the minutes each day at work.

With no motivation or desire to do anything positive for my well-being after work that day, I eagerly retreated once again to my cozy, brown leather couch after eating dinner. I contemplated how I have tolerated this state for so long and what I could do to change as I lazily browsed a celebrity magazine. Further distracting from my emotions, I zoned out watching ridiculous but entertaining reality TV, mindlessly snacking on salty potato chips, and feeling a stomachache coming on. This seemed easier than taking action on my self-improvement and being conscious of my feelings. Self-consciousness and self-doubts often kept me from even going out most days; I had a deeply-perceived need to hide.

Years of depression, frustration, acute loneliness, and overwhelming debt led to dark and terrifying thoughts of snuffing out my light. I thought taking my own life would be easier and it wouldn't really matter anyhow. I felt like I couldn't talk to anyone about these thoughts (and was shushed and dismissed when I finally opened up to a couple people about it). It took a long time to realize I didn't actually want to die (which took reminding when those thoughts crept in and they got very loud). What I really craved was joy and love. I truly desired feeling sensations of excitement waking each day, seeing the first hint of the sunrise through my blinds and hearing the birds sing their morning songs. I wanted to glide through my day with confidence and high energy even when life's challenging hand of cards were dealt because I was powerful, resilient and enough. I envisioned my slightly crooked smile, the sparkle in my eyes and hearing my laughter as I engaged in conversation with a close friend or my mom, instead of regurgitating negative stories and spilling fears and tears.

I was always questioning what was wrong with me and not good enough about me. I had very low self-esteem and self-confidence even when I was highly complimented by friends and strangers on a broad spectrum of my gifts and beauty (gifts and a unique beauty that I did not allow myself to see). I no longer knew who was looking back at me in the mirror.

Who was this green-eyed woman staring back at me?

One frosty winter evening, after another long day of work, I was fed up. A fiery rush surged over every inch of my body, screaming that I could no longer go on like this. Years of forcing and grinding through right at my edge, with a dysfunctional and suffocating existence, was having its way with me like a crazed ragdoll in this explosion of emotion. I could no longer tolerate my way of being. Aware that I was sitting within the four light tan walls of my cozy living room decorated with my rustic shabby-chic vibe, I had lost all sensation of safety, comfort and cognizance of what was happening. My breath escaped me, and I fell into a defeated heap on the hardwood floor, hysterically sobbing. I heard moans and wild crying I didn't recognize from myself, from a woman I didn't even recognize.

As I lay on the cold floor, a grounded calm was rising from my gut. My soul was whispering to me that despite the pain, this was the next and greatest step in my journey towards evolvement, freedom, and healing. In that very moment, I decided to sell my home, leave my corporate job, and move to the northwoods on Lake Michigan where I'd always dreamt of living.

I wanted to finally love myself for who I authentically was and have full belief that "I am enough." I was ready to explore myself honestly through a lens of love rather than loathing, and stop hiding through the years of abuse, being alone, and feeling so scared and lost. I wanted to live on purpose and stop giving such a massive fuck about what others think of me.

No one has witnessed my deepest breakdowns or detrimental behaviors, or heard the relentless flood of harmful thoughts I battled consistently each day. I was exhausted from years of resisting what I desired because of fear and bullshit excuses (aka getting in my own damn way), hiding my authenticity and light, people pleasing, and performing. I also carried the fear of my own disappointment on top of what I perceived as others' disappointment and judgment of me.

Three months later, my feet unbearably sore from packing for weeks on end, I had unpacked my whole life into my bright new apartment. Wildly tall trees thick with leaves danced in the wind outside my windows, backed by an epic sunset. This was my new peace and beauty moving forward after my last night in my old house. Between excitement and anxiety, I'd gotten no sleep camping out on my air mattress. I'd driven away from the home I'd known for 13 years at 4:30am with hot coffee in hand, feeling a mix of exhilaration and fatigue swirled with fear and joy. I had left everyone and everything I knew, the largest independent leap I'd ever taken. Yet I had a beautiful fluttering in my heart. I couldn't quite believe it was real.

I wanted a deeper level of healing from these and other painful experiences because they kept resurfacing as soon as I thought I had a grasp on it and had moved on. I had gone to therapy, talked to my closest besties, was battling persistent dark thoughts of taking my own life trying to replace them with positive thoughts, journaled and engaged in activities to create more joy in my life, which all seemed like smoke and mirrors because I still felt so depressed. It wasn't enough; I could feel in my bones there was something huge missing. It was forgiveness and acceptance that were missing. To finally decide to release anger and resentment.

Over the last several months I had started into my personal journey of life coaching. I was desperate to feel better, and have more happiness and peace in my life. I knew I wanted and needed a deeper level of healing and understanding with myself. It was like the excitement of fireworks when I felt the sensation over my entire body telling me this was the right and very best way for me to embark into coaching. It was not only to learn how to better create and manage my own emotional wellness and live a life I desired personally and professionally, but to inspire others into action to create a better life with a solid belief that they are enough. I was starting to feel new and powerful shifts within myself with what I was learning, doing the inner work of coaching myself and other coaches, and transforming every single day. I was building self-belief and self-confidence with such vulnerability, grace and compassion. My desires to have more in my life had come to full realization that evening I broke down on the floor, and I then made a firm soul decision there was zero turning back from.

I had made a choice, despite the fear, to follow my soul and have my own back. I had no one to fall back on, and there was no turning around. I was choosing to love myself more powerfully and with more courage than ever before. I was releasing the old stories and limiting beliefs that weren't serving me. And I was doing this all with belief that I could, without any evidence yet that it would all be okay. I was trusting myself, but also that God had me in His hands, no matter how choppy the waters would become. I discovered that the choppiest waves were the thoughts in my mind, and that they could derail me fast if I allowed them to.

Forgiveness (forgive, not condone, there is a difference) in order to move forward in my life, heal, and to release the feeling of actively reliving the horrible moments of my life in daily anguish when things felt too hard, lonely or painful, and too in relationships, was essential. Ultimately, to forgive myself for thinking that maybe I somehow deserved the beatings and the pain because I wasn't pretty, thin, smart, or good enough and to drop the damn shame that's thick as molasses. I carried such deep shame from it all. Most important of all in this healing of forgiveness was accepting and loving myself unconditionally regardless of my looks, body shape, material possessions, financial status or what someone else's idea is of good enough. I forgive it all because I know that woman in those moments was not the authentic, soul-level divine woman that I purely am with zero question, nor did she deserve any of it. No woman or man deserves to be beaten or abused.

I have reflected so heavily on past relationships with men and friends, and there are so many harmful situations and patterns that I endured because I didn't think I was good enough or mattered enough for anything better. I didn't believe in myself. I can now absolutely recognize I was not loving, respecting and honoring myself nearly enough, if at all. I did not respect and value myself in a way that would teach others to treat me that way as well. We teach others how to treat us by the way we treat ourselves. I relied on humor, self-depreciation, over-drinking, and binge eating to get through these painful and destructive relationships and experiences to avoid feeling and to numb-out.

It took me many years to discover that I am an empath, especially when I felt such an abnormal and unpleasant drain in energy. I can sense emotions amongst others around me and I absorb them, and they become deeper with more direct connection with their energy. I genuinely care about how people feel, and this can be intensely overwhelming on top of my own emotions. Many may not understand what an empath is and how it can feel. I indulge in joyous and upbeat energy of others. It's infectious with satisfaction and dizzying excitement with our laugher, wildly entertaining thoughts and spontaneous adventures as we dance within each other's energy. However, it can reach a point of being too much. It's like a concentrated high I feel head to toe in my body; it's very addicting and I never want it to end. I start to feel a sense that I'm out of control and am in discomfort noticing I'm out of alignment with my own integrity and personal energy levels. It impacts my thoughts, heightening them to the addictive high, as well as the negative lows. I too easily take on the negative emotions as my own, and that really weighs on me. Great bodily and mental awareness is needed to know when I need to pull away from the situation and the people to recharge because of the abnormal drain. Places such as concerts, events with a lot of people and bars are powerful source spots.

I am also an introvert. I absolutely love going out and being social, laughing until my cheeks hurt and relishing in my wild side, whether at big events or small! It's just my reality that the energy can shift to a point that isn't serving me and I'll recognize this, and I thankfully know how to care for myself to recharge. A flirty, fun-loving, spontaneous and social introvert on top of being an empath means for me that I need alone time to recharge doing things that realign me and replenish me such as hiking, journaling and sometimes simply sleeping.

Due to the negative and self-limiting beliefs I had about myself and those I took on from others throughout my life, I radiated this unconsciously on an energetic level. Even though I would have such exciting, blissful times and have a heavy sense of humor, I unconsciously emanated a solemn and disconnected mood most all of the time. This all further perpetuated those dark thoughts that creeped in that I no longer wanted to live, that that would just be easier. I just wanted the pain and suffering to stop.

I believed there *must* be some way to feel better at a core level, and I would hunt it down even though it felt so very far away. Love is my M.O., that is my core. It took nearly my entire life to realize the core of *me* was exactly what I truly desired the most: love. Not the perfect body, house, man, friends or job. I wanted to love myself.

My own love, compassion, forgiveness, acceptance, and my own healing and freedom from these heavy, unbearable chains—love is the ultimate gift I can ever give to myself or to anyone.

And come to find, these heavy, unbearable chains were self-created.

I am still discovering many things along my journey of healing and self-love that bring clarity to actions, behaviors, and thoughts that cause certain feelings and results, and how that carries over into different areas of my life and causes undesirable impacts. Because I desire evolvement, love, healing and joy, I continue to explore myself with curiosity and no judgment. I long for affection, passion and intimacy deeply, because that is my nature.

How you do one thing is how you do everything (in relationships, career, money, health, and spirituality), a concept I learned a few years ago through my coaching studies. Such as, I notice how I half-ass certain things or start something and never finish but usually have the same damn excuses amongst them; I connect these dots in all areas of my life. The most liberating part is when I'm able to identify the root of a pain point. Exploring the root with raw honesty allows me to feel through it, forgive and release it, and choose a new thought and new behavior to live as the highest version of myself. Acknowledging the thoughts and beliefs I have about the root cause, and having the power and freedom to choose new thoughts and beliefs that serve me and make me feel how I want to feel, is the pure magic of transformation. I must truly know myself in order to change myself. I am constantly learning, changing and becoming more resilient and self-confident. I am certain the true healing comes from loving myself unconditionally and releasing judgment. Even the parts of me I don't always like, by fully believing in myself and having conviction that I am enough, worthy, deserving and lovable just as I am. The sheer fact that I am alive is being fully enough, worthy, deserving and lovable, and nothing can add to or take away from that. I simply am, period. You simply are as well, period.

My journey of self-love the last few years has been such a wild, beautiful ride with no shortage of breakdowns, obstacles, panic-button-oh-shit-worthy moments, as well as an abundance of such peaceful relief, personal freedom, and blown open awareness. I've evolved into a new version of myself experiencing deeper breakthroughs. All the while I've walked through the scary to get to the other side of my fears and doubts, even when they are still present, and always will be. I'm creating so much personal power, self-confidence and the deep love I've been seeking so desperately for over three decades—my own love. No one can fill that but me. I also discovered in loving myself that my pure light and love is the energetic vibration that I am putting out into the Universe to call true love right back to me.

I may not always like myself, and I experience negative emotions when I'd much rather not, though it's an inevitable part of the human experience. We wouldn't know the good without the contrast! With the transformational work I've done on myself and continue to do daily, it's a powerful shift I am able to create. I can free myself from a dark rabbit hole of judgment, self-loathing, negative loops in my mind of untrue beliefs and stories that I tell myself because of that well beaten path in my brain that I've created by thinking these things over and over and over. This is ultimately from being disconnected from love; I can create my freedom instead of staying stuck there.

I now have the insight that the negative emotions are not only completely normal and expected, but they are feedback and clarity for my evolvement. The obstacles that arise are detours that are guiding me in the right direction along my destined path. Sometimes not liking myself is okay. This allows room for expansion and new levels of love and compassion, while carrying a deep knowing that my love for myself is unwavering. I am not broken and splintered; I am whole, but have lived in fear and judgment instead of love. Love always wins.

When I'm feeling out of alignment with love and joy and am instead living in fear and judgment, I can feel the heavy swell of it clouding me mentally, emotionally, physically and spiritually. I take it as a cue to create a "cocktail" of noticing what I am thinking and why and how it's making me feel. I step back from my situation or emotion to be a calm observer in order to gain pause and perspective, while mixing in compassion, curiosity and releasing judgment.

The hasty tendency to judge myself (and others, which is living in fear, ego and judgment instead of love... and yes, we all do it) and wallow in a depressive state of miserable thought loops on constant replay is a disconnection from love. So is unconsciously embodying a victim mentality perpetuating everything by being blind to it, as well as making untrue meanings and beliefs about myself. It feels horrible; it is literally a horrible physical and emotional discomfort that I displaced blame to some other cause for it. Had I been connected to and operating from a space of love this would not have been at play, even unconsciously. Indulging in emotional eating and these patterns of suffering had been my defaults when I have been out of alignment being disconnected from love. When I am living in fear and judgment, and feeling sorry for myself, I am choosing wrongly to stay disconnected and out of alignment. I repeat—I am *choosing. You* are choosing.

Being connected to love is where my purest warm light glows and it guides me, always. Because it is my soul. It is a choice to operate from loving soul energy over a tainted, bruised ego. I never realized before it's a choice—I always thought life was happening *to* me. I didn't know life is happening *for* me. Nor did I realize how to differentiate between soul and ego.

I have choice at my disposal at any given moment. I am the creator of my experiences by deciding how I want to think and feel. Regardless of external circumstances I cannot control, I still get to decide how I think and feel, even with the most terrible incidents. Some moments are easier than others to reconnect to my soul, but the shift is quicker and more resilient each time. I am more conscious to what I am feeling and experiencing than ever before. I have awareness that when I am not feeling well, or there is some sort of contraction or friction between what I feel and what I desire to feel, I know to explore my thoughts and observe them. This is always the first step to my inner work because determining what I am thinking clarifies why I feel and act the way I do. Then I can further discover my thoughts and shift how I feel.

Often times we aren't aware of what we are even thinking; we think over 60,000 thoughts a day! Our thoughts create our feelings. Our feelings determine our action, inaction or reaction, which then determines our results. A result that often is not desirable when conscious, intentional and soul-aligned actions are not taken. It's about leaning into and feeling the emotion instead of ignoring it and having destructive reactions to it; to allow it to be present, acknowledge it and honor it for what it is, and release any judgment on it.

There is no healing in judgment, force, or punishment. I've tried for endless years and that's never the answer. There is, however, healing in love, compassion and curiosity, and having a willing heart to explore myself. It's a deep exploration identifying what my fears, judgments and beliefs are. And, if my beliefs are true for me now or if they are what were programmed into me as a child or someone else's I took on along the way that I do not even want to own or believe any longer. I also explore if those beliefs are even serving me or not. I allow full surrender to vulnerability, not to show me my weaknesses under a microscope to analyze, but rather to expose more clearly my strengths, gifts and how courageous

I truly am. If you're desiring changes in your life, you first must know yourself in order to change yourself.

The process of releasing what no longer serves me has been so wildly pivotal in my continued renewal. This includes releasing and shifting thoughts, beliefs, stories, behaviors, relationships and parts of my identity that aren't authentically my identity. This ability to create space to allow in the healing, receive with an open heart and giving even more, having greater joy, and better overall health and enjoyment with movement is invaluable. Getting into nature and really being present in it, cherishing and deepening my connections with others, relishing my time in my fave coffee shops and on my much loved trails or waters, experiencing more peace, and stepping up to have the willingness and desire to change destructive behaviors is such a beautiful, healing and fascinating place on earth and within myself to be. It's also discovering a zest for life I lost, or possibly never fully had, and have the taste now of how phenomenal this really is. I continue showing up for myself even when I'm tired. I listen to my body when it truly needs rest instead of choosing to quit, and when I feel overwhelmed or tired, I still commit to my movement for my mental, physical, emotional and spiritual health.

Now if I begin crying wherever I am-in my truck, walking along the bay in my hometown or the beautiful downtown streets with gorgeous hanging flower baskets in the summer or white lights intertwined in every tree in the winter, an epic hiking trail-I allow it for healing. I do not dismiss it or tuck away the root cause. Dismissing and avoiding only perpetuates the suffering and intensity. I allow myself to feel it and become the observer of my thoughts. This is the root of any emotion I have—my thoughts. To create real change that will last, instead of using force and willpower (which isn't sustainable), find what you love, what brings you energy and joy, and actually *do* it. Not just thinking or talking about it and allowing day by day to go by feeling shitty knowing damn well you have the power and authority to do something about it! For example, I've recently lost 30 pounds by doing things I enjoy and by observing and changing my thoughts with my coaching expertise.

It doesn't mean I always have something to fix or change, though sometimes it does. It doesn't mean that something is right or wrong, or good or bad. It's about whatever meaning I'm making of it and knowing that the way that is best for me is based on how I want to feel and liking my reasons. It doesn't mean I have to stay with the same thought, belief or behavior if it isn't serving me; I am allowed to change and can think or believe or do whatever I want regardless of anyone else. When I am trusting myself coming from a good place driven by my soul, I am at peace being authentic and true to myself, and again liking my reasons. What's beautiful is that you always get to choose what you want to think or believe—no one can take that from you.

I'm choosing to create healthier, happier and more fulfilling experiences for myself by not staying stuck in the same destructive behaviors and dysfunctional patterns I've played out for years. I have thankfully and considerably learned, been deeply pained and forever enlightened from them. I'm refusing to live the same patterns day to day as if they own me, feeling like I'm on a leash being drug through each day stripped of my own authority. There are ways to make it manageable in small steps for lasting transformation.

The first step is acknowledging what you feel, deciding you want to feel better and love yourself, and choosing to commit to that. There is not one damn thing that is selfish about that! Drop making some reason or "rational excuse" that it is wrong or not ok. It isn't selfish or wrong to want to feel better, love yourself and to take action on that! Make the decision to step into your power and own it.

The next step is deeply thinking about what you want in your life and why. Why is it important to you? What do you think you will feel in having it? And if it's so important to you, why don't you already have it and where are you stuck? Journal it out without editing or judging yourself; get really honest with yourself (again-don't judge!) and explore. This brings clarity to what you want to be feeling, and what actions you can start taking now to create what you want. The needle mover for your desired changes is to actually take action. Not to think about it, wish and dream about it, but to start taking actions now that support and align with your desires.

The third step is to have your own back and show up. Show up for yourself and impress yourself! That's right, how about deciding to impress yourself and show yourself just how fabulous you truly are?

You are allowed to change.

You are meant to change.

Like your reasons for your desires and changes.

You do not need anyone's permission (though you'd appreciate their support) to feel better and love yourself.

Deciding what you want and having belief in yourself that you are capable to change starts to shift your energy into this transformational space. Allow the knowing that there is abundance surrounding you if you're willing to just open up and receive it.

This was the root of my problem; I didn't believe I could be her. She was too far out of my reach, out of my league. The lack of belief in myself by being energetically tuned into and acting out from so much deep-rooted fear and judgment, instead of being tuned into and operating from a place of love, compassion and my soul, fueled this destruction for decades.

The genuine release is letting go of the layers of my identity that were self-created with delusional fears, beliefs, judgment and deep trauma that was dismissed by numbing out and avoiding what I really felt. It isn't about shedding the actual pounds in weight loss, or thinking I'd feel better just swapping negative thoughts for positive thoughts for example. It goes much deeper into identity and beliefs. There is no healing in judgment and fear, though I didn't yet know that, or why, until I began my coaching journey and started peeling back these layers and getting honest AF with myself. Becoming the calm, compassionate observer of my thoughts while releasing judgment allowed me to step back to gain perspective. I observed my behaviors and emotional childhood (not taking responsibility for myself and acting out in ways that didn't serve me) of the younger version of me, and the many varying versions of me throughout the years as my life played out. With this compassion and a willingness to become conscious of how I had been operating over time, this is where the healing truly began.

I listened to what those many different versions of me wanted to say; those parts of me that were screaming out to be fully heard and acknowledged. I honored their pain, discomfort, fear, and frustration. I had to seek and acknowledge what the positive intention was for all of this madness. It was, even though in a seriously clusterfucked way, for my protection. I had not yet discovered a better solution that felt "comfortable" enough to manage my emotions, thoughts and circumstances in life.

Our primal brain wiring has us avoiding pain, seeking pleasure and comfort, all with as little effort as possible. Our primal brain hasn't evolved in the way that modern life has. There is no longer a threat of having to run from lions and hide in a cave to survive. However, that same fear response wired within is just as elevated today by things such as working a job feeling overwhelmed and stressed, having an argument with someone, or irritation from crazy traffic. There are endless factors and circumstances in life that we react to by seeking and indulging in comfort and pleasure to avoid what we are feeling and thinking. This keeps us stuck in primal patterns and avoids addressing the root cause. Most always we are just reacting on autopilot to what we are feeling with very well-worn patterns without first stopping to acknowledge what we are thinking that is causing the feeling in the first place.

Journaling, meditating, getting into nature and getting movement (yoga, hiking), working consistently on my mindset and beliefs, investing in myself with coaching and continuing my self-coaching work daily are essential actions in my process of renewal, clarity and healing that I've been sharing with you.

Are fears, judgments, and doubts still alive within me today? Of course, because of the well-worn paths still within my mind. Though I continue paving and following my newly created paths. Do dark thoughts still creep in? Yes, and they may always be there in some capacity, but I know how to quiet them when they try to get loud and get my attention. It's tolerable and I've accepted it all, because of the new created paths, thoughts and beliefs that serve me instead of destroy me. I'm no longer constantly so terrified and suffering out of control from it all because I love myself unconditionally and believe in myself with full knowing that I am enough. I know how to create and manage emotional wellness.

The discomfort of exploring and unpacking all of this to produce the much desired and needed shifts in my life is far less discomfort than staying stagnant and complacent in my self-created hell. There is always discomfort in change, and too there is discomfort in staying the same and becoming worse. There's inevitably discomfort in life and we are meant to experience it, so why not be the best version of yourself? You'll be in discomfort anyhow, so choose to do things that are aligned with living as the best version of yourself.

Which discomfort will you choose?

Choose your discomfort.

I choose mine.

I can finally look in the mirror and love the green-eyed girl looking back at me. I love the woman that I've been for her resilient journey braving the wilderness to evolve and heal and keep going, the beautiful, powerhouse woman who I become each day fully owning her worth, and am over the moon about the even stronger powerhouse woman I have yet to become. I now live on the inside looking out, because it's all within me, never outside of me. It always has been. I was simply stuck in my own whirlwind of drama in my head and hadn't yet fully opened my eyes or my heart.

The sweetest pleasure and most rewarding transformational shift has been the liberation I've experienced by choosing to love myself through it all—the amazing, the gruesome, and the in between. I have had my own back and stopped the extreme, destructive loathing of myself. I have learned to practice self-love, and finally accept that I am enough just as I am.

I finally love myself. And so it is.

Looking back at the younger versions of me so lost and hurt without the comfort she needed, I can now comfort and heal her. I remind her:

In the morning when you awake
Leave behind what you do not need to take
Look ahead, as far as you can see
Now go, even further, to be where you want to be

In your heart you will keep all that is true
In your mind you will see and learn all kinds of new
Grasp what you can and hold it tight
You may never come across something else so right

Melt in the sweetness of the shimmery glow
Smile, eyes closed, for the love that you know
Hold your head high and remain so strong
Do not let anything make you do wrong

You see above you the never-ending sky
You are part of its light that will never die
Dance through the sunbeams running through the tree's leaves
Blow wishes and dreams in the air and breath in deep
In any time of your want and need
Turn around and you will see
With a soul full of faith and an honest smile there I will stand
Reaching toward you with my soft open hand

THE JOURNEY TO INNER PEACE AND SELF-ACCEPTANCE

By: Kristin Larsen

The constant banging and humming of robotic, massive machines resonated in the background of the factory. The same physical motions of installing the parts on the vehicles as they moved along the conveyor, repeated over and over. The vehicles were arriving in the same spot on the assembly line every minute. My job was to install part after part on each vehicle as it came through with demanded perfection every time.

As a worker on the vehicle assembly line for 17 years, I had to sacrifice my body and my mind in order to meet the expectations of me. Conforming to robot-like movements, there was no time for emotions. Just perfection. Being on an assembly line, I never truly felt human. I never felt fully alive. I felt like a machine.

Sometimes in life we don't know the answers. We may be confused about what direction to take on our journey.

It is at this point of confusion where we can acknowledge and accept where we are or resist and fight each decision, choice and action we take.

My choices led me to work at a job in a factory, which, by its very nature, cultivated and accentuated two major struggles of my life: self-judgement and perfectionism. This job brought questions of "being enough" to each task I performed. My idea of perfection was the only standard with which I measured success because that was the standard others used to measure me.

Perfection and self-judgment made me feel incarcerated in my job and in my life. The solitary confinement in my mind always made the voice louder, crisper, and clear. I always remained a prisoner in my mind.

Reliving the same failures and enduring the same insecurities.

Worry and doubt followed me wherever I went, with whatever I did. I had a complex filtering process in which I constantly questioned whether I was doing something correctly. Was I saying something correctly? Was I interacting with others correctly? Every moment I would ask myself these questions, but the answer was always no, I wasn't doing it correctly. I began trapping my voice inside so I wouldn't be judged for something that might be viewed as wrong. I could never be myself. I didn't know what "myself" even was. I didn't know how to express myself without my own judgement or perceived judgment from others.

I could never live up to my own expectations. My perception of what I thought were the expectations others had of me made my self-judgements even worse.

I would silence the voice by suppressing my feelings. I learned to become numb to everything by hiding inside myself and my outside world. I thought it would reduce the possibility of judgements.

I would always ask myself the question, "How did I get here?"

But I could never find an answer. Then the most important question:

"How do I get out?"

A labyrinth of thoughts and emotions would follow. A maze inhabited with confused pathways.

The struggle was real. The suffering felt never-ending. Survival was the only thing I had known.

Every situation would lead me further away from freedom, inside the maze of judgement.

I thought, if only I had known the answer of how I had gotten there, I would know the answer of how I could escape.

I remember basking in the sun as a young boy. Just thinking about creativity and fun.

I was just being outside, enjoying the natural wonders of life.

Many moments like these flooded my memory as reference to what I grasped as grounding me to my reality.

I remembered family gatherings, playing outside in nearby fields and forests. Always making the most of and appreciating what I had in my life.

There was so much creating and imagining in a life full of possibilities. And at some point, creativity and imagination were replaced by self-judgment, self-doubt and worry.

As I grew older, learning became a challenge. It proved difficult to stay focused.

I began to label myself a below average student. My comparison to others started to intensify. It seemed like my results and efforts were never as good as others.

This became my belief. Tests were a struggle. "Why can't I remember anything?" I'd wonder.

I watched other classmates and friends accomplish more. "Why can't I?"

It was discouraging. "That must mean I am not as smart as everyone else."

I continued to tell myself that learning and school would always be a challenge for me.

I began to associate failure with school. Everything I did was either a success or total failure. I never felt like I was enough or did enough. No one else pressured me but me.

My earliest memories from public school were being disciplined for not listening or not playing "properly."

My interpretation was that I couldn't follow instructions the right way and I did things wrong. That would be the start of how I perceived my life.

Over time, I tried different things to invite more responsibility and learning into my life. I had a paper route. I cut lawns.

It felt good and brought me joy to help others.

Life also brought a strong need for belonging and a sense of identity. My sole purpose became to belong and fit in. Despite this, I continued to carry the label of failure and not being able to do things correctly with me each day.

But I continued to try things I didn't think I could do, or enjoy.

One such thing was public speaking.

I could always feel my face igniting into a warmth that was uncomfortable and uncontrollable. The only relatable feeling that comes to my mind is fire. My voice would begin to shrink. The more I looked at the bodies and eyes staring at me, the smaller and unworthy I felt in that moment.

It felt like I was failing, and so, another belief was imprinted. I was not worthy or enough to share my voice.

I began to accept that being quiet and deflecting the spotlight were the best strategies to fit in and belong. Embarrassment and red became a new feeling of colour.

Self-criticizing was my way of assessing life and judging each interaction. What I wasn't doing in my life. Who I wasn't being. A way to compare. A measuring stick of my worthiness and being enough.

The warning signs were always there. I avoided social contact for fear of judgement internally and externally. I felt sorry for myself daily. Anxiety and depression became my everyday acquaintances. I would walk around, thinking every person I passed was watching, staring, judging. I felt a deep sense of loneliness and isolation, which is the lens through which I made my decisions.

I remember in high school walking down the hallway. I thought everyone was watching me and staring. Judging me. I thought I could read minds. Their thoughts appearing visually to me. "You are walking alone. You are a loser. You are not enough as you are."

You can't do anything right. The delusion kept escalating until it was unbearable.

My answer was always to hide. Keep my head down and pretend I was invisible.

Insecurity became my daily routine.

Through various moments I began to believe in myself. Each small step I took every day, every week, every month, created more belief.

I observed how other people experienced various moments in their day. I knew I wanted to change what I wanted to experience. As I took in what others were doing, I noticed something began to change inside me. I started to improve my self- care. I began exercising, learning about self-esteem. I began to alter the tyrant voice that destructed my inner harmony.

Quite often I felt I had no skills, no future.

What I thought was my worthiness actually determined how I set my limitations in my life. Everything I experienced was a way of measuring if I was worthy of being enough. It was always a comparison to accomplishments or others. I thought that determined my value.

My experiences created my perception that people did not like me. I didn't fit in.

I formed many negative beliefs from my experiences.

I started to believe that I didn't take criticism well. I was no good at many things.

My skills were very limited. People were always vindictive. I was a failure if I couldn't keep up to expectations. Anger and resentment towards others helped me feel better about myself.

I used a barrier, a wall, a shield to prevent others from invading my inner psyche.

Keeping others out and not connecting deeply meant I could be in control of my internal pain.

As life continued for me, I discovered that the barrier I placed around myself prevented me from connecting to myself and others. I wasn't able to co-exist in the human experience with others. It was a lonely isolation.

I constantly worried about whether I would escape the prison I was living in. I lived in the doubt of ever being enough as a person. I would come home from work and suppress what I experienced through my day, then do it all over again the next day.

Other workers on the assembly line would often complain about their jobs. They'd say how miserable and lifeless it made them feel. I didn't want to be like that. I did not want to live like that.

Instead, I constantly judged myself for being in the position of having this job in the first place.

Each day I would go to work with hatred for what I was doing. Then I'd count down the minutes until my day would end. I felt like I was a failure in life to be where I was.

Internally, I felt paralyzed. Each day I repeatedly thought about dying.

Every few months I would experience a wave of depression. I could feel it coming and just got used to it. I would slowly feel it make it's way into my life. I would brace myself for the downward spiral of thoughts and emotions I was about to experience. I thought that being a man meant I had to be strong. Showing my suffering would mean I was weak.

So, I chose to suffer in silence. My ego was all I had left to help me survive and get through the day. Hide the weakness to avoid the judgement and pain.

I wrote a poem which encapsulated the mental challenges I was enduring each day in my life:

Walls enclosed into me; Vines tangle my mind, suffocating my soul, unable to breathe.

Struggle and squirm, diminishing senses, blind to see. Tired thoughts, and slumber dreams.

Drowning spirits, silent screams. Time moving forward, but out of phase. Staying afloat, for another day. Ambushed by distancing thought. Concluding the improbable. Expecting an illusion. Maintaining the delusion, to endure the blindness. Awaiting the cage to be lifted, believing the mind will be free. Carrying the soul, for many promises. Seeing reality, through my eyes.

One day, following a bout of extreme perfectionism and self judgement a single conversation changed my thoughts and my perception of how I was experiencing my life.

I knew I needed help, at least someone to talk to. I met with a therapy counselor and discussed my "need" to be perfect all the time. They said, "So, what if you're not perfect?"

I thought, "What if I'm not perfect? What would that mean?" It would mean I could be enough.

Whatever I did would be acceptable. I wouldn't need to meet unrealistic expectations in order to be worthy of anything I was doing in my job or life.

When the meeting with the counselor ended, I walked out the door lighter, like a weight had been lifted off me. I decided to give myself permission to let go of the constant unachievable expectations I had been placing on myself.

I began shifting how I wanted to experience life.

Through past life experiences I had learned that travelling opened a gateway to creativity for me. I felt a sense of connection to myself, others and the world when I traveled.

I felt alive when I saw all the intricate details that surrounded me in life. It brought wonder, curiosity, exploration, and a new found freedom. Most importantly, I lived in those moments without judgement and perfectionism.

I desperately wanted to make a statement to myself and the world to shed the self-judgements and perfectionism and welcome my new identity into the world. I wanted to start a new life with new outlooks.

Gradually I learned the importance of connection to myself and others.

Traveling allowed me to see the beauty I didn't know existed. It helped me take steps outside my comfort zone in my life. I began initiating conversations with others, letting go of all the self regulated rules and strict expectations that I needed to adhere to in order to be enough. Creativity and curiosity fueled my desire to learn and grow without judgement of failure.

When I experienced deep love in my relationship I learned how to be open to give and receive love. I witnessed the importance of trust, honesty and forgiveness. These values helped me to be more present with my feelings. I began to place focus on what brought me joy. It opened my eyes to see the unique beauty in others.

New choices and more opportunities began to appear in my life. The possibility of leaving the prison I felt trapped in for many years became a new reality.

In ten years I experienced many highs and lows in my life. I travelled to many places.

I visited England, Scotland, Italy, France, Germany, Netherlands, Czech Republic, Luxembourg, Denmark, Sweden, Portugal, Spain, Costa Rica, Mexico.

I also bought my first house. Then I married someone very special who offers joy and aliveness. Life is always an adventure with her. Moments I always look forward to and anticipate.

I have learned so much from her. What it is like to be full of energy, to be alive and so giving of self to others. To be yourself without worry of judgement. To be free from perfection and allow others to see your character for what it is.

I was determined to start making drastic changes in my life. Stop letting self-judgement and perfectionism rule my life. Get out of the waiting stage in life to start creating opportunities.

I decided to start a business that combined my love for traveling and the outdoors. I continued to take steps as I pursued that dream, I began attending business workshops and seminars.

I attended a small business workshop that was hosted by a reputable public relations consultant. I was excited to get information that would help me move forward with my business.

At the workshop, I was confronted with the legitimacy of my business plan and foundation of my business.

The brutal honesty of the consultant stung. The consultant delivered their perspective as sincere as they could. "I urge you to stop operating your business!", "Stop investing your time and money in this.", "There is no future in this.", "Think about what it is costing you in your life."

I had thought this was going to be my future and that I would evade the self-judgement that had been following me my whole life. Instead it created more confusion about how I could be worthy and enough in my life.

Despite the difficult choice I had to make, it was time to accept where I was in my life.

We were expecting our first child and it was no longer just about me. Each day was a responsibility to be there for my family. I couldn't do that if I was wallowing in my own self- pity.

There were some prominent reasons why I was able to get through the dark times.

First, I surrounded myself with many supportive and encouraging friends. They were so full of life, kindness, and appreciated each other like family. They were like my family.

What I had was a strong bond of closeness with them. They illuminated the grey inner world that would often accompany me in life. I truly felt like I could be myself without judgement or perfectionism around them.

I began creating opportunities for myself that would be in service of self-care.

When I placed more attention on proper sleep, exercise and nutrition, my energy changed. My mood changed. The insecurities of perfectionism and self-judgement were reduced.

I also learned how to release my emotions, which eliminated much of the shame and guilt I had often experienced.

A moment comes to mind when my Nan (grandma) passed away and I was asked to deliver a eulogy.

I stepped onto the podium and for once in my life, I was not nervous. I wasn't thinking about myself and the perfection I needed to have in order to convey the messages I wanted to share about my Nan. I wanted them to know about the love, hope, kindness, and giving she brought to the world and to the lives of others around her. It was the first time I cried as an adult in front of others. I wasn't afraid or ashamed to show my emotions. I wasn't scared to show how much I deeply cared for her.

It was freeing for me to celebrate her life with others without holding back for fear of judgement. I realized not only was I mourning her loss, but I witnessed myself release my own suffering that day.

From then on, I began to build resilience in my life. For example, I had always wanted to run in a half marathon. While frequently enduring leg aches and pains, I wasn't sure if it would be a good idea. "But why set limitations on myself?" I thought.

I trained for months. Running every other day. With my hips and knees aching, I completed two half marathons. I pushed myself more than I ever had in my life. I was content with doing the best I could, not with what the results were.

I was proud of myself that I finished any race, let alone two.

The birth of our two children also brought a new placed significance in to my life.

These miraculous human beings required my love and affection. It helped me to see life in its truest form. No judgement or perfection. Just worthiness and being enough. Just love and acceptance.

I looked at my skills and interests. I looked at what I could be good at and opportunities I could create. I volunteered in the community, developed my writing skills through a children's literature course, designed games, and learned about internet marketing. I no longer focused on expectations; I was in a place of creation.

Despite all my progress, I could often feel myself move back into a dark place again. I started to have more worries, doubts, and insecurities about being a good father, husband and person. I never realized how depleted energy and sleepless nights impact one's mental state.

I began to feel nervous in social situations again. I was always trying to plan what I would say or do. Nothing seemed natural. Everything seemed forced.

Nevertheless, I kept continuing to grow as a person even through anxiety, perfectionism and self-judgement.

I loosened my grip on the pressure I was placing on myself to leave my job.

Even though my body was in constant agony from work.

Despite being mentally and physically exhausted daily, I held a place for gratitude.

I took moments in my day to be thankful for my job. How blessed I was to have a job.

Even though it was a job that was unfulfilling for me, it provided opportunities for my family.

I also realized there were worse situations I could be in. When I stopped struggling with where I was, or what I was doing, my perspective changed.

I was no longer focused on not being enough or living up to my own expectations. I was grateful for what I have and the life I am blessed with. I was in the midst of my journey and wherever I was in that journey, there was no wrong place in it.

My life changed again one day when I typed the phrase, "finding purpose in life" into an internet search on my computer.

A video came up as a search result.

It was a TED Talk by someone named Scott Dinsmore. He explained about his journey of changing careers. He later called "doing what you love", "Live Your Legend."

I then clicked a link that said, "learn how you can live your legend."

I enrolled in a program that helped me discover more about myself and help me explore purpose.

It brought clarity to what my values, interests, and what brings purpose to my life.

A contest was promoted which encouraged me to start a blog. The winning blog would receive complimentary entry into another course program called Connect With Anyone. The program helped with understanding how to connect with others and self.

As I entered the competition, I wasn't worried about the perfectionism and self- judgement that had plagued me. I just wrote. I expressed myself. I learned how to be vulnerable to reveal my true authenticity. It helped me maintain my focus on what I wanted instead of placing guilt and shame on what I didn't have, what I wasn't doing, or who I wasn't being in my life.

My blog was chosen as the winning blog. I had the opportunity to enroll in the course.

I practiced being authentic while connecting with others on a deeper level.

During the course each person was placed in a mastermind group.

Through regular meetings the group provided support, accountability, and acknowledgement of the journey.

The journey took me through exploring writing, and many other creativity projects.

Through the shared mastermind group experience I found my desire to help others while using my creativity and imagination to be a very high expression of enjoyment.

I found that my own self- judgements, questions of worthiness, doubts, and worries began to slowly subside. It was because I was connecting with others. I was having the opportunity to share in experiences and not be isolated in my own experiences.

I learned that it wasn't what you were doing that brought fulfillment in life. It was who you were being every day that brought fulfillment in life. I didn't need to leave my current job to experience being enough to meet my own expectations.

I continued learning more about myself and through research I found that coaching matched all the values I wanted to incorporate into my life.

I decided that all my interests, experiences, values aligned with health and life coaching.

Through continued research I chose to enroll in a coaching program offered by a school called Health Coach Institute.

After completion of the one-year program, I was officially certified as a health and life coach. But I didn't want my journey to end there. I enrolled in a mastery coaching program and continued exploring my deep inner beliefs and how to change them.

What I learned about myself required courage, empathy, self-compassion and most importantly, honesty with myself. Having presence with myself and giving myself permission to heal.

My self- concept of my experiences continued to change. I didn't have the need to view myself as broken or feeling isolated in my suffering.

When I removed the protective barrier that I had formed in childhood, I shifted my focus to living with an open heart. I accepted that by embracing my imperfections it helped others feel more comfortable about revealing their true self. The self- judgements I held so tightly were let go and replaced with presence, empathy, compassion, curiosity and gratitude.

What I realized was it wasn't about the journey of trying to find purpose in life to be enough or worthy. It wasn't finding a career that would bring me fulfillment. My experiences were trying to help me embrace self- acceptance.

Happiness was not something that I could create on the outside. It was something I created on the inside.

I had been so concerned about completing whatever I was doing in life and not taking enjoyment in the moments that were needed to get me there.

What I learned about happiness was that it is not defined by having a certain job or career. It wasn't about something specific that I was doing. It is who I am being each day.

For me it is being open, connecting, authentic, full of love.

I didn't need to have judgment of my thoughts or feelings. I can choose to let go of the need to be in an obligated mood of happiness every moment.

It was unnecessary for me to prove my worth to myself or others. I am forever worthy and enough as I am.

Thirty-two years later, I found my way out of the maze. I realized the exit was always near me. I just chose not to see it.

Each belief I formed throughout my life also accompanied a story. The story would continue to evolve into my perception of reality. What I believed is what I viewed in my life.

What I saw in my life is what I believed.

What I learned was that I have the choice to choose what I want to believe. This means I have the choice to choose what I see. My perspective determines my reality. If my perspective determines my reality, then there are infinite possibilities and choices available to me that I can't see or don't even realize yet.

I choose to see love. I choose to see kindness. I choose to see compassion. I choose to see hope. I choose to see possibility. My beliefs form my reality for what I want to see.

I often thought I needed to do everything on my own. I needed to overcome all obstacles and challenges myself.

How I arrived at this moment in my life was because of support, asking for help, and connecting with others who shared love and kindness with me. It may have been a word, a conversation, or a simple gesture that helped me continue my journey towards where I placed my focus.

I had created a protective shield around myself all my life to avoid hurt or pain.

I had suppressed my feelings to become numb to continued thoughts or emotions of suffering.

The internal critical torture was often unbearable. Reliving moments over and over.

Internal scrutiny for every detail or possible outcome. Why I didn't choose another option.

The comparison and measurement to my results.

I needed to give myself permission to surrender, to stop resisting and fighting. I needed to start accepting where I am in a given moment and acknowledge that it is okay. I will be okay.

Detaching from my ego allowed me to surrender completely. I stopped numbing and started feeling. I started being present with my pain. Then I could have the choice to let it go.

I let go of evaluating my life based on results. I replaced the evaluating with curiosity and intention. I embraced the learning that comes from each situation which helps me to appreciate and enjoy each moment. I allowed presence to replace the doubts and worry without basking in permanent judgement.

Presence and gratitude allows me to detach from judgement when it does appear.

I place focus on functioning in life within my values to continue moving forward with trust and belief in whatever I am doing.

I have freedom when I detach myself from what I am holding resistance to.

My will to survive was the dedication and appreciation of my life to be free.

When I forgive myself, it is the kindest act of love as I embrace self- acceptance.

I found that gratitude is being present to the appreciation of being alive. Acknowledging the value of the shared human experience.

I came into this world as a small baby desiring love and connection. I realize now it doesn't have to be more.

My new story I choose to live in thought and feeling:

I am enough for who I am because I have compassion and empathy for myself and others.

I am imperfect and accept myself for my strengths and flaws. I am worthy of having inner peace and happiness because it is rightfully mine.

I give myself permission to accept outer happiness because I am grateful for being me, and for the life I have.

I am loved and have priceless value in this world.

I am irreplaceable. I trust and believe in myself so that I can have courage to learn and grow without attachment to an outcome.

I AM FREE.

LITTLE LIES: WHAT KEPT ME STUCK IN ABUSIVE PATTERNS, DISORDERED EATING AND PEOPLE PLEASING DEFAULTS

By: Katelyn M. Flores

It was summer in the 90's. I was an attractive 13-year-old in middle school, the oldest of three children. We lived in a popular and progressive city in Massachusetts. Nirvana and the Backstreet Boys were all the craze. We used scrunchies in our hair and wore bodysuits with jeans and Keds. TGIF played on TV every Friday night, Jonathan Taylor Thomas was the hunk of the century, and Fridays were the highlight of my week. We loved watching shows like Beverly Hills 90210 and Baywatch, especially when Mom and Dad were not home. We were required to go to summer school, not because we had bad grades but because we needed to be active.

Mom always used to say, "I don't care what you do, but you're going to do something during summer vacation."

On this particular summer day, we were home alone for a few hours after summer camp until mom got home from work. This was not the norm, but she was starting to trust us more. Our eyes fixated on the television, watching the forbidden Baywatch lifeguard show and eating mac and cheese. Not the powdered cheese kind, the good kind—the one that came with an oozy cheese pouch. Gooey, golden, Oozing, tangy, cheesy liquid gold. My favorite "food."

On this day, the liquid gold seemed irresistible, like cake on your birthday or a cigarette after a nice stiff drink. As I sat there, staring at the TV, I consumed every last morsel of the liquid gold, spoon to mouth, mindlessly shoving it in even though I wasn't actually hungry, getting a delectable "hit" after every bite. I ate until my belly hurt deep inside, reeling in discomfort. It was the uncomfortable dull ache of a belly three times too full that felt like it was going to burst. My younger sister, the thin athlete, scolded me and told me I was going to be in big trouble because mom would find out I ate the whole box. I was scared of the impending wrath and undeniable shame from my mother, so I anxiously and quickly conjured up a way to hide the evidence.

Moving more quickly than my legs could carry me and faster than my brain could process, I buttoned my pants back up and hid the mac and cheese evidence—the little cardboard corpse and the pretty silver cheese pouch, stuffing them in the trash. I shoved everything back in its place, even reorganizing the dishes in the dishwasher so that it would not be detectable that there were added dirty dishes. Once I was done with my shenanigans, I assumed my place on the couch like a good girl next to my siblings, waiting for mom to barrel through the door, pushing down and ignoring my belly pain, even "sucking it in."

To me, this was the perfect comfort combo: forbidden fantasy TV and my favorite "meal." This day seemed different though, something had changed when I finished eating. I remember reeling with discomfort next to my younger brother and sister, watching the sexy Pamela Anderson dressed in a red thong bathing suit with handsome male companions frolicking down the beach, life float in hand. I wanted to be like her, a blonde bombshell and bouncing boobs. I had never really noticed her in that way before, but it was as if a light switch turned on and all of the sudden, I knew how "not enough" I really was. I didn't know it then, but that liquid gold experience, using food like a drug, became the gateway drug to other foods and became my novocaine for life. I didn't even know I *needed* novocaine. I just knew eating more than my belly could handle felt good.

I remember being at the birthday parties of friends with hokey pokey blaring, strobe lights blinking, children screaming in joy, and all the other big feels that adults seem to forget little ones have too. I always hated those parties. They felt like a record that had reached its end and kept skipping. I felt it inside my body and it consumed me, sending me into a whirlwind of people pleasing, ignoring my own feelings and taking care of everyone else. I would often tug at my mom's shirt, look up at her, and ask her why people in the world seemed so sad. I wanted to know more,

I wanted to uncover the root cause and fix their sadness, even as a pre-teen. I was ignoring myself, my needs, welling up into an anxious mess of body image issues, self-esteem problems, and an eating disorder in the making.

Food became the one and only thing that quieted the noise in my mind and stopped the record from skipping. Eating fixed the loud noise in my head like nothing else had before. I can remember another food experience, being as young as six or seven years-old at one of our Halloween parties. My parents threw fun parties with activities like bobbing for apples, dancing donuts you had to catch in your mouth, and potato sack races. At this party, I was in my hand-me-down costume that my siblings and cousins had worn ten times over. It was too big for me with faded colors and missing the red nose. My friends wore new and fancy sequined costumes of gold and turquoise adorned with shiny beaded trim, *with* the magic wand in hand. I wanted their costumes and their rich dads with the nice shiny cars. It all seemed so perfect, and I felt like a peasant. I too wanted to be able to eat the sugary, fatty, tasty foods that their parents allowed them to eat. I wanted their lives, not mine.

At this particular party, I ran into the house crying because I was so overwhelmed with all of the children and expectations that came with having 10 screaming kids around; I didn't want to hurt anyone by hitting or saying mean things, I hated it when it came to that. When I went in the house, I was followed by a parent and scolded for being an "ungrateful little shit." I was told to get back out there and "be kind to my guests." My parents or my guests, didn't know my little feelings were squashed like a bug, that I felt smaller than a shriveled pea and that they scared me to my core with their words and presence. When around my parents, it felt like my feelings didn't matter and I knew that, loud and clear. I wanted nothing more than to crawl into a hole and die than to be responsible for all of those people and their *big* feelings. Despite how I felt, I headed back outside, with a forced smile strapped on my delicate and tear-soaked face, terrified of myself and all of the energy around me. As I matured, those experiences of chaos, overwhelming moments, insecurity, and using food to relieve my mental anguish continued to repeat in my life and paved the way for the gradual downward spiral of my self-esteem and sense of well-being.

At the dinner table, whenever any of us kids didn't "like" what was being served, the usual response was, "I don't care if you like it or not, you will eat what is on your plate or you will not eat at all and you will go to your room, and I don't want to see any crying about it." We learned really quickly not to verbalize any opinions about preference, ever. Mom was not a stay at home mom; she worked full time. Despite her hustle and harsh approach, mom's meals were always tasty and wholesome. My friend's moms made them boxed and frozen meals. Not us. Mom worked in the food industry so she knew what kinds of foods would make us big and strong with functioning brains. She would tell us that a balanced meal of protein, starch, and vegetable was essential for healthy living. My mother made a balanced meal for us every single night of the week. Most things were made from scratch. Pork loin, peas, and mashed potatoes was one of my favorite meals; I could have eaten that five days a week. We called it "P, P & P night." We rarely ate things out of boxes, from the freezer, or processed. If we did, it was a big deal and considered a one time "treat." There were "treats" in the pantry like crackers, chips, and cookies, but those were to be earned and eaten in moderation with permission from mom or dad only.

The confusing part was that my mom was overweight my entire life. She was always struggling with managing her weight. When I was around 10-years-old, I would see the Red-and-white checkered Weight Watcher's cookbook in the pantry and feel her disappointment and anger that she couldn't keep weight off as she got up before the kids to walk several miles at the park. "It's our genes, we are all overweight on my side of the family, some people are just bigger," she would assure me. Sometimes my aunt and I joked about our "gene pool," blaming our big butts and thighs on the "gene pool."

Mom thought she hid her struggles well, talking on the phone in secret, going for long drives by herself, rolling back into the driveway with glistening flushed cheeks after crying and red eyes, with the Patsy Cline quietly playing the background. We could feel the tension, hear the contradictions, feel the sadness, and see the lies. I think my mother really believed that I couldn't see that her face was red, her eyes were bloodshot, and her heart was broken after her long solitary drives "to the gas station." I always knew it was total bullshit, feeling the pulsating sadness of her heart, but I kept it tied up in a bow for her, because if she knew that I knew, she might break. I always knew my mom was sad and overweight and sometimes I fantasized about having a mom who was slender, like the mothers that my friends had. I wanted it for two reasons: I wanted her to stop suffering and I wanted someone I could be proud of and tote around like a prize. I didn't want to witness her trying to cover up her tremendous shame when she didn't fit in the auditorium seat at our performances, spilling over on to the others.

Physical appearance became important to me early on, much like a child who grows up with an alcoholic parent and vows to never drink—I never wanted to be fat. I understood its importance and felt how it demanded attention; MTV showcased Pamela Anderson, Mariah Carey and Britney Spears and I knew in my heart if I just worked hard enough, I could be "pretty just like them."

My mom often reassured us that she was eating balanced meals, even though we knew it was a lie. When we were in the car, I found bags of potato chips in the back seat and candy wrappers stuffed in the back of the driver's seat pouch. If ever we spotted a junk food wrapper, we were to promptly look away as if it never happened, knowing full well that we shouldn't "rat mom out." I knew that mom had a problem with food, but I wanted to protect her from shame and humiliation, so I kept her secret for her. I innately knew that within my family system, my mom's shame and guilt would likely kill me if I "outed" her. So, I held the shame in my little heart in a tiny box with a pretty bow, letting it ferment and fester. I protected her even if her actions didn't match her words and hurt like a vice grip squeezing my heart.

We kept up appearances and facades well, but my mom couldn't always keep it together. She crumbled sometimes, sobbing, hitting my dad and telling him to stop drinking, which he did regularly. Dad's drinking effected his relationships with his family, especially with my mom. Dad and I never developed that fuzzy father-daughter bond that I always dreamed of. He always seemed too far from my reach, never being fully present or engaged in my life. My mom and dad's "love" felt more like scrutiny and angry forced words in lieu of loving nurturing action. Dad thought he was a military captain and mom thought she was a tough love guru. We kids sort of "manned up" in order to cope. Strangely, I knew mom couldn't help but be in a constant state of anger. I overheard the secret stories of she and her seven siblings fending for themselves like orphans left to their own devices, hardening to the world. Mom seemed like an insecure child, grasping desperately at a sense of "normalcy" for herself and her family.

I was at the pediatrician's office one day with my mom. They had one of those large fish tanks with cool colors and creatures in it. I remember gazing into the cool, steely, blue, water, mesmerized by the shapes and the reflections on the other side. I always loved water—swimming in it, playing in it, and understanding its power. On this day, I remember asking my mom why a girl was crying across the waiting room. My mom gave me a generic answer and kept reading her magazine. I was locked on the girl. I couldn't stop watching her and feeling her every move. She had tears coming down her pale cheeks, wearing Oskh Kosh overalls with brown little pigtails. She was sad and no one seemed to be doing anything about it.

I tugged at my mom again, and said, "Mom, that girl is really sad, we have to help her." My mother took a little more time and explained that she had a mommy who was taking good care of her. But I couldn't let it rest. My heart became heavy and all I could see was the suffering girl, disappearing through the fish tank as we were called in to the exam room by the nurse. The Osh Kosh girl was sad and she needed help, no one was helping her. I had to help her. But I couldn't; I felt like I had failed.

I was mad at the inability of the humans around me to truly care for one and other. The stirrings of distrust in my heart had begun. These stirrings emerged very early on in my tender life and I didn't know what to do with them. The visions and urge to help others was like being offered a handful of tasty candy from the neighbor that I knew would poison my belly, but I ate it anyway. I stuffed the confusion inside my body, my bones, and my soul, reeling on the inside and displaying an accommodating smile on the outside.

Although I had found food and begun to depend on it for emotional release, I maintained a healthy weight throughout high school. I developed early with full breasts, hips, rearend, and an hourglass figure. I was starting to look like the women I adored on TV. But I despised my butt. I *hated* it.

My body hatred started in second grade, around eight years-old, when a little girl changed the ideas of my body forever. We were playing our favorite kickball game with the maroon squishy kickball, splatting against the concrete wall, seeing how hard we could make it "splat." When it was my turn to kick the ball, one of my friends said, "You have a big butt," and ran away. I felt my senses prickle up instantly, hair on the back of my neck rose and a hot flash of adrenaline surged throughout my body. I instantly retracted and got small, although I was trying to brush it off. I told her to "shut up" and kicked the ball like nothing happened. My face was red with shame plastered all over it, my little heart pounded, and I instantly tied my flannel shirt around my waist to cover my butt. I was mortified. I knew we had big butts in our family because of the "gene pool" jokes, but I didn't realize it was *that* big. I wanted to run home from school, the five miles or so, and never return. I fantasized about having a rich mom who would allow me to do home schooling and buy me all of the school clothes I wanted. I decided I must have been defective and that I didn't look like the supermodels after all, changing the way I saw my body for the rest of my life.

After that, I got small, quieting my voice, not taking chances and playing it safe. I *never* shared my opinion unless it was asked for and I tried to blend in the best that I could so that I wouldn't have to explain myself or my position. I started wearing oversized flannel shirts and obsessing about getting more shirts that would cover my rear end, crying if I couldn't find the perfect tunic that would disguise it. School shopping was an utter *nightmare.* The fights, tears, embarrassment and shame were always on full blast when it came time for school shopping. "Mom, can I have just *one* pair of Abercrombie pants? I will wear them three times before I wash them, I don't need any other pants, I promise," I would beg. I insisted that we get the expensive clothes that would efficiently minimize my rear.

During the transitions into another school grade, in the hot days of summer down-time, I also started gravitating towards the music of the 90's. I started hearing and feeling the lyrics in a way I never had before. My veins pumped the depressing lyrics throughout my body. "It's rain on your wedding day, it's the good advice that you just can't take…" Alanis Morrisette was very popular then and I *really* felt her lyrics. Music was a big part of my family, and went generations deep. My grandmother always sang her sentences and my mom harmonized to every song she heard. I willingly embraced my beautiful soprano voice and love of music too.

"Kate, just sing one song with me, I am your mother, everyone loves it when you sing for them," my mother would plead at gatherings. Saying no was never an option. I hated singing on demand but I always did it anyway. Despite my expression through singing, the food still called to me and nothing took the edge off of my anxiety quite like food did. I continued to eat for comfort and relief, eating in large quantities when I could get away with it, especially at friends' houses. I remember delighting in soft, delectable Twinkies, hearty canned-beef stew and count-less hot pockets from the freezer at their houses. Despite my growing uncontrollable sadness, I kept smiling on the outside.

As life pressures continued to pile up, my focus was on how to keep a thin body and still eat large quantities of food to relieve the stress. I also started another odd and neurotic behavior: I would gaze into the mirror at my face, peppered with nose-freckles, in my parents' room with the door locked. My parents and siblings were engrossed in their activities, paying no attention. I remember feeling a sense of release and relief as I plucked out my eyelashes, in clumps, with my bare hands. When I got a good clump, I held them in my hand, examining them up close, perseverating on the tiny white roots of my lashes in awe. The more I could get, the better. And oh, how sad I felt when there were none left. The urgent feeling in my chest and head of "more more more, more is better," played over and over. I didn't know where it was coming from, why I did it or how it started or even that it was "bad." I just knew that it was strangely satisfying, plucking the eyelashes from my eyelids, watching them pile up, feeling that sense of accomplishment and relief. I used to play a game and see how many baby eyelashes I could get from the very inner corner of my eye, even though those hurt the most. Each pluck felt eerily satisfying and satiating.

The eyelash pulling was a way to commandeer my life into beautiful distractions so that I wouldn't have to deal with what was really churning underneath. Things happened when I was a small child that would later make sense of my odd behaviors. One day, it dawned on me— the memory surfaced. I remembered that as a young girl, I had been molested by my uncle. All of the self-abusive "behaviors" fell in line, like perfect missing pieces to a puzzle. Eyelash pulling had become a temporarily successful way to hurt myself before anyone else could and a way to control my body before someone else did. I thought I hid my eyelash pulling from my parents, but my mom walked in on me one day. I was mortified by the shame and guilt that once again ravaged my little body and I stopped out of fear. I fell in line, once again, vowing to *never* to upset anyone with my needs or desires.

In high school, senior week was a big deal. All of the hallways were decorated with festive party favors, music, streamers, and crazy scenes for senior week. Someone even had a dry ice machine. Everyone was high on adrenaline and competing for best hallway. The hallway colors were muted browns, oranges and cream colors, typical of the 90's and the school store was hopping with commerce. The old lockers creaked and were dinged up from years of use. The entire school buzzed along like a city of it's own. As older girls walked by, they shouted at me, "SLUT, WHORE!" Boys snickered and muttered, "Wide load" under their breath as they walked by me. I pretended it didn't crush me and I hung with the "cool" mean girls despite their torment.

This was before the term "bullying" was popular and before any administration really did anything about it. This was pre-Phoebe Prince, the 15-year-old Irish teen who killed herself on January 24th, 2010 by hanging, as a result of relentless slut shaming and bullying. I remember being in school, walking to math class with my paper covered text books in hand and hearing the news of Phoebe Prince.

A wave of panic swept over me as I thought, "I wish it had been me. I wish I had the guts to do it." It felt especially close because she only lived a couple of towns away. After Phoebe died, I felt numb and frozen, completely understanding why she did it and fantasizing about doing it myself. I knew the feeling of desperation and sadness, I knew suffering and wanted to feel relief too. I felt jealous of Phoebe Prince for having the guts to kill herself.

Throughout high school, even though over eating was my thing, I quickly realized it wasn't useful if I wanted a hot body. I went through anorexic and failed bulimic phases with the intention to change the shape of my body, specifically my butt. I went days without eating and only drinking water. Sometimes, my friends joined in and we considered it a sort of competition.

"Meet me in the bathroom after homeroom," they would whisper to me over our pile of backpacks on the homeroom table. JLO, TLC and Boyz II Men were in, and so were "big butts" and the hip-hop rap craze. The eager and willing boys enjoyed my curvy body; blue eyes, full hips and thighs, small waist and dark hair "yo, can I get a pice of that?!" they would yell as they passed by. They were always older than me and with that, came a greater sense of responsibility and pressure that I wasn't ready for.

I remember one of my older boyfriends pleading with me "Come on I saw this on a video me and the guys were watching the other day, Mark did it with his girl, it will feel good try it," as he tried to force me to have sex. He pressed up against me, ignoring my uncertainty and "no," causing me so much pain that I disappeared, like a cloud, floating above my body. I hovered over my body and took a virtual field trip around town until it was over. I had been told about sex education in school; the sperm and the egg and tampons and stuff, but I was only 13, I didn't really understand it and I was too embarrassed to ask. And I knew that if I said "no" that the boys would leave me and find someone who said yes. "Maybe this is what they all do and what it feels like for all of the girls," I thought. "I guess it's not that bad." I started doubting my feelings and intuition and feeling like it was not safe to have my own vulnerable feelings because they would just be ignored. I had to borrow the *proper* feelings and social cues from others. I was starving myself and being bullied by the girls during the day and fending off the boys and their friends on the weekends. But I never told anyone.

As the pressures of high school grew, so did my food addiction and obsession. I loved eating things like prepackaged cupcakes, chips and any forbidden foods I could get my hands on. I developed a scarcity and deprivation mentality through my "dieting," and I got *really* good at putting off pleasure for "later." I could hold out on eating until the big reward. I starved for days and then gorged on whatever I could get my hands on, like a starved dog.

I continued to eat for comfort. At dinner, I asked for seconds and sometimes thirds. My mother always rationed our food and always monitored our food intake.

"Kate, that's enough, your sister is still on her first serving." I never *could* live up to my perfect and obedient younger sister in the eyes of my parents. I never dared to ask for more than thirds, so I would wait until after dinner. "I will clear the table tonight," I declared, partially out of sense of duty and partially driven by my desire to consume. After dinner, my parents went into the living room to relax after their "long day," while we volunteered for chores and did homework. As I cleared the table, I shoveled bits of mashed potatoes, dinner rolls and butter into my mouth, with one eye still on the living room to make sure no one saw me, listening for footsteps from around the corner.

I was always on edge, waiting to be caught doing something wrong. We were never caught doing something right, so, I learned how to self-preserve and remain on alert for a potential threat constantly. I tried to anticipate the feelings of my parents and siblings; were they happy, sad, angry, mad? "Ooo, they are in a good mood today," I thought. "I might be able to get a few more minutes alone," I would think to myself as I stuffed my face with leftovers. But, the second I heard someone coming, I threw down what I was eating and sometimes even went into the bathroom to finish chewing so that I wouldn't get caught. Getting caught felt too scary. At the same time, *not* feeling relief from the anxiety, doubt and insecurity felt just as scary, so I battled out the consequences quickly in my head. To eat or not to eat?

There was a big cardinal food rule in our house: if it was not already open, you were not allowed to open it without the permission of mom or dad. So, if no one was paying attention on my way through the pantry, I would take out anything that was already open and shove it in my mouth. It didn't matter what it was. I was always counting the minutes until someone caught on. Sometimes, when everyone was asleep, I would go downstairs "to the bathroom" and spend 15 minutes standing at the pantry counter shoving down chips and other treats, opening them ever so carefully so that my parents couldn't hear me though the heat register that went from the pantry to their bedroom. It didn't really matter what it was as long as I got the "fix" I was seeking (which never came). I often ate the entire bag, usually potato chips or Smart Food popcorn. I hid the bag in the trashcan, under other trash. But my mom usually knew. Of course she did, she liked food too. She knew the tricks. I got caught a few times and scolded by her. "Katelyn, what the hell are you doing down here?"

The embarrassment of getting caught, the shame, and the guilt oozed over me like molten lava and my heart jumped out of my chest. It felt like a prickly rash that I couldn't scratch. My mom really knew how to pack a punch when she came down on you, with her tone and expression alone. The shame of getting caught permeated through my heart like a permanent dagger, forever lodged inside. I vowed to myself never to feel those feelings again. I never wanted to disappoint my mom, but the drive to eat for comfort and relief felt irresistible, like the sweet smell of a new baby to a mother, or a sip of water to the desert. It soothed me, temporarily.

The drive to consume food strengthened over time and it was like I couldn't control my own hands, they involuntarily reached for the snacks on the way to the bathroom. "You are so stupid Katelyn, stop eating like this, you will be as big as Mom," I thought to myself. Yet, I couldn't stop. When I realized I was no longer in control of my behavior around food, when I started feeling like some other motor was driving my brain, I got really scared. But I knew what to do when I was scared. I got creative and learned how to open the chip bag ever so quietly so I wouldn't get caught. I learned how to tiptoe throughout the house lightly and which parts of the floor to avoid so that it wouldn't make the telltale hardwood creaking noise. I learned which foods to eat first and which foods wouldn't seem so obvious if I ate the entire thing. I ate the old foods that had been sitting in the cabinet for weeks, half eaten. I knew no one else was going to eat it, and therefore not miss it. I got smart, just like any other addict would.

For a short time, I played lacrosse in high school. But as the pressures of high school socialization requirements grew, I quit the lacrosse team, against my mother's wishes. I was more interested in the fast life and being popular. Not long after quitting, I became destructive and self-abusive, *very* quickly. "Hey, Hailey's sister can get her hands on some vodka, want to come with us to her house this weekend?" I started getting my hands on alcohol, crashing parties when the parents weren't home and spending entire weekends "away at my friend's house." "Mom I'm going over Hailey's house and I'm sleeping over tonight." My parents weren't tthat naïve, they always spoke to the parents first. After my parents confirmed with the other parents, we took off into full party mode! The parents were *never* there, or if they were, it was only during the day. They lied for us, wicked awesome parents! When I was not home, my friends and I were basically free-range teens with bottles of liquor, marijuana at big fancy houses with pools and hot tubs. I loved the freedom I had to express myself and be included.

This trickery on my parents continued throughout high school and I got caught a few times. I learned that it was a lot easier to fit in with "bad crowd" because they weren't picky as long as I was going along with the plan. I desperately wanted attention and validation and I did whatever it took. I wanted to feel love, so I played the part I thought I needed to play in order to be accepted. "Hey, want to go with me to Sara's house and get a bag of weed?" I didn't even like the stuff, but I went anyway. I always knew it wasn't the real me and felt conflicted.

The voices in my head told me, "Katelyn you really shouldn't and you don't even want to, but they will like you better if you just do it, you won't get caught." I faked it for so long, ignoring my intuition, that I lost all concept of who I really was, what I believed in, and what my values were. I became a submissive chameleon and blended in with whoever would have me at the moment. From the hardcore gangbangers to the patchouli-wearing hippies and everything in between. I desperately wanted to be seen, yet hidden tightly in a bud all at once.

I was obsessed with appearance, body checking in between every single class. I had favorite bathrooms, mirrors and stalls and rushed to get to them when the bell rang, negating any socialization in-between classes. "I'll meet you in class," I would yell over to my best friend. I hid food and threw it away often, restricting and depriving myself. It worked, it kept my weight under control, made me dizzy and desirable. I even tried to purge, shoving my fingers down my throat in the school bathroom, but I didn't have a strong enough gag reflex. I tried a toothbrush, that didn't work either. I even asked a friend to help coach me through it, but I still couldn't get it up. It became harder and harder to starve myself and the drive to consume remained deeply engrained. I craved my comfort foods and wasn't getting any relief from restricting. So, ultimately, I reverted back to over-eating and binges.

Although my parents told me with their words that they loved me, it was not always apparent. I was often told by my mother, "You are just too sensitive Katelyn, stop being so dramatic, you need to get thicker skin," as she tried to prepare me for the harsh world. Sometimes things got pretty heated between us. One time, while in the pantry, after "getting a snack" after school, my mother slapped me, and I slapped her back, food in hand, after I probably mouthed off to her "for the last time." Sometimes she held me down on the couch and would recruit my father to come help. It seemed to me that my mom was starting to become unable to discipline me on her own because now she needed my dad to help her. I felt like I was finally winning.

Until she said things like, "That's fine, Miss Smartass, if you want to continue to act like this, your father and I will send you to boarding school." This terrified me but I never really knew what it meant. I just knew I would be "sent away." I was terrified to be sent away to a place where I imagined they would hit me with rulers and lock me in a cobwebbed attic with no food or water. But I knew that even if I had to be sent away, I would make it. I knew that I had a fire and fight inside me even though I constantly felt like I was living a life that wasn't mine. So, what was one more chapter in the life that wasn't really mine? I could do the boarding school time, I knew I could. I braced for it, for the moment when mom and dad would sit me down and tell me it was time to pack to be sent away. Thankfully, that time never came.

"KATE!" my father's voice would blast through the house, quivering just enough that we knew it was business. My dad was not a very expressive man, he was more stoic and withdrawn. So when he yelled one of our names, the world stopped. When we heard that distinct quiver paired with the volume of his powerful holler, it meant it was big time trouble, probably the belt. We went running, reluctantly, to our inevitable punishment. "Pull down your pants" he would say. We resisted but eventually did as we were told. I don't remember how many times we got hit because I became the cloud, and dissipated into the atmosphere, floating in a sea of eerie and lonely anxiety, high above my body, waiting for it to end.

To cope, I made it into a game sometimes: "Let me see if I can *not* cry this time, that will *really* piss Dad off." I held my tears tightly inside as they morphed into rage and thought of other things like swimming in the pool or what I would eat later. My siblings, and sometimes cousins, if they were visiting, were always so afraid. So I took that on too, protecting my siblings pleading, "No Dad, hit me, not them," while standing in front of everyone, arms spread out like barriers, wings of protection. I felt like Jesus on the cross, bleeding, wearing a thorn crown, waiting for the lashes, to spare the others. I learned quickly how to brace for the strike of the leather belt or the hand and "take it like a man" and then move on with my day. Almost like nothing happened.

By some universal miracle, I graduated high school and went off to college where things rapidly got worse and alcohol became another addiction in tandem with the food. I remember being drunk, with a clear glass of straight-up vodka by my side, crying to the soft sad sounds of Norah Jones all by myself in my single dormitory room, the campus dusted with a fresh white snow and the yellow glow of the campus lights. My hot face stained by black mascara and old eyeliner from the night before, my belly bloated and my hair on top of my head in a messy bun. That miserable internal record played over and over in my college days. "Seriously? I could just end all of this bullshit once and for all, and I know how I could do it..." were the consistent thoughts that bounced around in my skull. I never mustered up a solid plan or intent at this point, and instead, I stuffed the desire to die into my bones where it festered and soaked right in.

As I continued to stuff my feelings, an unexplained widespread body pain started. The doctors told me I was too young, that it was stress and that I needed to manage my stress levels. I went to countless therapists and doctors all of whom could not figure out what was causing my body pain. Some called it Fibromyalgia and degenerative disc disease, offering me narcotics for pain management at age 19. I refused the medications that I knew would offer me nothing but a crippling life sentence of drug addiction.

At my university, there were hundreds of students in each auditorium-sized class. The campus was so big that it was easily a mile walk to some of my classes. I found some familiar friends from high school and created a "tribe" of sorts that felt safe. At the beginning of the year we all went on Weight Watchers together. We weighed in weekly and shopped for low-point foods. We worked out a lot, binged on alcohol at night and cured our hangovers by eating very large portions at fast food. The hangover-binges felt hot, sweaty, gross, and strangely satisfying. I continued to drink and go to parties, barely making it to classes. Eventually, my learning really started to be affected by my lifestyle. I was sent to see the campus psychiatrist. I was diagnosed with ADHD, major depressive disorder, PTSD, OCD, and anxiety. I was also tested for a learning disability. My school could not confirm a conventional learning disability but awarded me a note taker and extra time on tests. They concluded that that my "alcohol-induced psychological conditions" were considered a "disability." I stamped myself as a disabled loser and kept it moving. I hid it from my smart School of Business friends and tucked my head down in shame.

After graduating college, I got a decent social work job with the state, but it didn't quite pay all of the bills. So I also worked at a local jail and domestic violence shelter, working 3 jobs, building up my resume experience. I didn't realize that life could possibly get harder. In 2010, four years after graduating college, living alone in a large, high-crime city, I was violently sexually assaulted. I was held down by one man while the other man gripped my legs, pulling them open. I couldn't yell and scream, my voice box wouldn't work. As I kicked, it all seemed to go in super slow motion, never ending. The two perpetrators, local business owners with families, had likely done it before, as It seemed well orchestrated.

I told myself the assault was my fault and that I shouldn't have been wearing those sexy heels and form fitting jeans. I also couldn't fathom being publicly dragged through court. I pictured the heading in the newspaper: "State worker accuses local business owners of rape." I had completed 40 hours of domestic violence and rape crisis training that same year, so I knew what would happen and I knew the statistics. I also couldn't believe it happened to *me*. I *was* the counselor. According to Rainn.org, out of 1000 people sexually assaulted in the United States, 995 perpetrators will walk free. So, I fell in line, like most other survivors, and I didn't report it. It felt too risky. I called out of work for two days, locked my doors, cried in bed until my eye sockets hurt, and ate until I felt like I was going to burst. I told no one. I had bruises on my arms, puffy crying eyes and was bloated and hot from alcohol and food binges.

I felt even more alone than before. Like a corpse whose job was to appease the public, smile, nod and fall into the dark abyss at night, never to surface in true form. I felt like a useless wench of a woman who took up too much space on this earth and too much sacred ground. I felt trapped in my nightmare of a life, watching like a spectator from the outside and pushing three hundred pounds. The sweet voices of suicide crept back and whispered the naughty taunting words: "You can really do it this time, just end it, no one will ever love you anyway." I knew deep inside I could no longer withstand anyone's abuse, especially the abuse I put on myself. The constant torment of food, restriction, binge eating and drinking, working out too hard and repeating. Abuse, rinse, repeat. I lost my sense of security and sense of self. I wasn't sure who to be or what to become next. What would be quicker and less messy? A bottle of pills? Driving off a bridge? Hanging? Lethal injection? I thought, "I have some nurse friends, they could help with an injection," and even asked one of my nurse friends if she would consider it. I kept dragging myself through the mud, picking myself up piece by piece, leg by leg and moving on, utterly exhausted and deflated. At my job, I was a thorough, type-A, precise worker bee and a crumbling disaster by night.

"The Public Service award for 2010 goes to Katelyn," my manager read out loud as she handed me my achievement award. To outsiders, I was a champion, I always got it done, at any cost. The hustle was familiar and somewhat easy. The pain of the hustle and invalidating my feelings became comfortable and familiar. I hid all of this from my family and I never told them. I couldn't bear to disappoint them, and I certainly didn't want them to be right about me being too sensitive. What if this was just bad karma for being a "difficult" teenager as my mom always said? What if I deserved it?

Now, on Psychiatric medications to cope, feeling foggy and still living alone, my food behaviors continued. I often ordered out at fast food places. I ordered very large amounts of food, enough for five people to eat. I was seeking that familiar fix, release and comfort. I waited to get home to eat the food, side-eying it the entire car ride. I was able to temporarily postpone the pleasure for the ultimate reward at the end, when all conditions were in place. Doors locked, AC on, sweatpants on, TV on, blanket on, all food within reach, no one around and the phone silenced nearby as to not be interrupted but still connected. Everything had to be at my fingertips. I would eat three burritos, (not the wimpy burritos, the fat, dense burritos), two tacos, a bag of chips and chase it down with an entire pint of ice cream. Oh, with a diet soda too, not because of the calories but because I liked the hit of the aspartame on my brain. I had major GI issues and became dependent on laxatives too, needing two colonoscopies in my 20's. My body couldn't handle the volume and abuse, ironically, not one doctor ever discussed my eating habits with me.

My heaviest weight was over 260 pounds, at 5' 3". I could only shop at the "fat girl stores," the ones that had gaudy floral moo moo dresses in their windows, wide-calf boots and horizontally striped blouses on their shopping racks, as to further embarrass and shame plus-sized women. They didn't carry bigger sizes in the mainstream stores back then and I hadn't been able to shop at popular mainstream retailers for many years. I felt left out when my college friends went and splurged at the mall and I stayed home. It was too embarrassing to not be able to fit in "normal" clothes and come up with excuses as to why. It was strictly The Avenue and Lane Bryant for this size 22-24 girl. But in my mind, I was still attractive because I was recruited for plus-size modeling, cat-called by men and considered to be "curvy." I was completely confused, thinking my body couldn't have been *that* bad if men still wanted me. The truth was, they wanted to use me for whatever they fancied. I was an easy target, eager to please and they knew it. Most of the time, what I saw in the mirror was a distorted, smaller, fantasy-like version of myself. Maybe I was seeing a smaller version of myself because I was playing small in my life. I had become dependent on what others thought of me in order to decide how I felt about myself, not real facts or how I truly felt.

One day, my coworker challenged me to join the new Crossfit box that had just opened up down the street. Reluctantly, I agreed. The coaches there put me on the "Paleo diet." Completing my daily "WODS" and eating

Paleo, the pounds started coming off. I was kicking ass and taking names, deadlifting 230 pounds like a boss. I cooked pounds of bacon and meat in one sitting and drank coconut oil to increase my fat intake. I was trying to convert my body into burning ketones for fuel instead of glucose. I obsessively checked my blood sugar and ketone levels 6-10 times a day. One day, on lunch break, I came home from work to get my lunch. I started feeling woozy on the way to the house and had to pull over and vomit. I proceeded vomit four more times before I got to my driveway.

When I finally made it up the stairs, I collapsed on the bathroom floor. I was freezing cold but sweating. I felt like I was going to die. I remember thinking, "Okay, if I die, I did everything I could." I was vomiting and all over the bathroom and couldn't return to work. Despite my body's warning signals, I still didn't stop the diet or seek medical attention. The number on the meters, in addition to the numbers on the scale, told me how well I was doing on my diet, so I endured the discomfort. I became addicted to Crossfit. I lost 60 pounds, I was exhausted with adrenal fatigue, dependent on magnesium supplements, my hair was falling out in clumps and I had painful injuries all over, but I was losing weight. I couldn't see any of the destruction and none of that mattered because I was finally losing weight. My food addiction paused, temporarily, and shifted to exercise. I managed to keep the 60 pounds off with extreme working out.

I got confident enough to date again and I met a man. We fell in love and got married in dreamy Colorado. *But,* by the time the wedding came, my dress was too tight. I could barely squeeze into it. The stress of the travel and major life changes all at once catapulted me into full on binges again. I remember having bags upon bags of chips and junk food in our hotel room.

Every day that I walked in and out of work, I thought about how to end my life. I imagined it being the last day I ever walked in that place, with their standard issued government clocks that never faltered, the mismatched carpeted floors and the ugly gray cubicles lined perfectly in a row. I imagined saying good riddance once and for all. I was starting to make real plans and intentions to end my life and sleeping from the moment I got home until it was time for bed. I felt like I was lying to clients, sucking at being a wife and selling my soul to the devil by squeezing myself inside the governmental box that squelched all of my creativity. I couldn't bare the pain anymore. On the outside, I was confident, talkative and vibrant, so no one had any idea what was happening on the inside except my poor husband who worried every day. I made the heart wrenching decision to quit that job, leaving the pension, benefits and good pay. I knew deep down that I had to say yes to myself, not yes to a paycheck.

Eventually, I stumbled upon a 12 step program for people who are addicted to food. I didn't think I was an addict but it seemed like it might help. Reluctantly, I went to my first meeting, terrified and desperate. It was in an old dingy room at my alma mater, with hard folding chairs facing the speaker in a semi-circle, just like you might see on television. As an introvert, it was a very scary moment for me. Everyone's eyes were on the "newcomer." I don't remember much of what was said in that first meeting, I was too busy sweating, and alternating my uncomfortably crossed legs, worrying about whether or not people were staring at me and my stomach rolls. That night, I spoke to a woman who agreed to sponsor me even though she had a full roster. I had landed a good one. I started talking to her on the phone and texting her every day as instructed. She was intimidating, harsh, prestigious, and militant. I was also told I was in "the Marines of food programs" and that I'd better get my act together if I wanted to be of the elitist community. I thought she was what I needed, tough love, with a scared straight approach. I was actually very scared of her, and the fear kept me in line perfectly.

I thought more "treatment" was better so at the recommendation of my sponsor, I agreed to attend an additional meeting, an intensive study of the 12 steps. I hated attending meetings but dragged myself there 3 times a week after work anyway. This additional meeting had strict rules that prohibited me from taking my medication or drinking coffee as a condition of its membership. I had used food and my medications to cope with all of my emotions: happy, sad, bored, excited, nervous, depressed. Now, I had to have little bits of my "drug" three times a day in controlled amounts, unmedicated, while working two jobs that were killing me, in a new marriage and in a new home, with a new puppy. I wanted them to just lock me up in a padded room and leave me there. I remember in the beginning, I felt like a raw nerve exposed to the cold air and that I wished I were addicted to "hard drugs" so that I could commit myself to a facility and stop taking them and move on. Consuming prescribed bits of my food "drug" was excruciating. It was like telling someone they can have half the hit of cocaine that gives them the perfect high or 1/4 of the alcoholic drink that will lead them into euphoric bliss. I felt like a naked baby in an ice bath, too much torture to endure. Many members could relate with my stories and some just gave me lip service. I took it personally and I felt unsafe at times, like I was too much for everyone with all of my big feelings and that I had to censor my words, or speak like them. After all, we agreed in step six of the 12 steps that we were entirely ready to have "God remove all our defects of character." So I fell in line, walking the walk, and talking the talk. I completely rejected the word "God," replacing it with "universe." But I still understood that I was defective. Simply defective. That's all I heard.

As I gained momentum in the program, I earned my first 30 days, 60 days, 90 days and one-year recognitions. There are no coins to earn in this program, just verbal praise. I wanted a coin, I earned it! I became a sponsor too. I was able to do what we call "white knuckle it" for a year and a half. After my one-year mark, I made a choice to leave the program. I remained "sober" from food for 20 continuous months and haven't had a drink of alcohol in 4 years. Many people relapse within the first few months to a year. I held strong and clung to my tools like lifelines, blocking out all life around me. "Sobriety" and "abstinence" was my only life. A sponsor had mentioned that 115 pounds would be about right for my height. So my goal became 115 pounds, no matter what it took. In July of 2018, I remember looking at myself in the mirror, 118 pounds, my collar bones protruding, my hip bones jutting out and my face starting to look sunken in. Even though I monitored and reported my weight weekly, I felt like being thin snuck up on me and I didn't know where it came from, much like the 260 pounds came on in the first place. I knew for sure that I still wasn't seeing with my "real eyes." I was seeing through a dysmorphic filter, distorted and warped and I didn't trust what I saw in the mirror. Besides, I still had 3 more pounds to lose, so I wasn't perfect yet. I remember seeing my legs so thin that I didn't recognize them. I always hated my tree trunk legs, and now they were wrinkly sticks. I had done it. I was finally thin. The program had worked. But I was so thin that my friends and family were concerned and started discussing their concerns about my body size behind my back. I had no idea. I didn't see what they saw. I still saw cellulite, new face wrinkles, loose skin, saggy boobs and stretch marks.

Although it was thrilling and exhilarating to wear a size 4 and extra small, I was not happy at all. I counted the minutes to my next meal, obsessed about meal timing and what I was eating, scarfed my food within minutes, cancelled events and didn't book trips because it would interfere with my sobriety. I was good at obedience. I was an anxious mess, missing all of life's precious moments, but I defied the "gene pool."

My biggest fear was that I would binge again. To me, a binging equaled weighing 300 pounds and being on the road to suicide again. I was always told by the program leaders that the first bite and first morsel of something forbidden would equal me being "face down in the food." I feared that I could not control myself and get back on the wagon if I ate "off plan." Despite being my biggest fear, the "stomach bug" that I contracted in 2018, propelled me into a series of uncontrollable binges, each one feeling worse than the last. For a month, I agonized about not eating "on plan," wore nausea bands on my wrists every day, was pale as paper and unable to take in any "whole" foods like vegetables or lean meats without vomiting. I vowed to get back on track when the mystery stomach bug finally ended.

One night, I caved to the relentless callings from my brain to binge. I planned it just right. I waited until my husband got in the shower, I knew what I wanted to eat and planned it out in my head. Like a hardcore addict, I started shoveling food down my throat while listening for the shower to stop. I stood at the bottom of the stairs listening. My heart was pounding out of my chest with adrenaline, fear, guilt and shame. It felt involuntary, like my brain and arms were working against my will. I did not want to actually binge. Yet, it felt familiar and comforting. Even though I knew it would hurt and I knew it would send me into a downward spiral I kept going. My heart and belly said no but my brain and hands said more, more, more. It was *excruciating*. I had tears in my eyes and I was sweating, hearing my heartbeat in my own ears. I felt like a heroin addict, picturing the needle in my arm, envisioning myself slapping the inside of my elbow to awaken my veins, and seeing the addiction centers in my brain light up like a Christmas tree. It was an out of body experience. It was self-sabotage, abuse, and destruction and an end to deprivation. It was coping. It was comfort. It was long term deprivation and scarcity acting out in real time, getting its claws back into me once again. That binge caused me days of mental and physical pain.

Following that binge, I started to change. Something was shifting inside me, and I was beginning to reinvent myself. A phoenix rising started coming from within me. It too felt a bit involuntary like something that was creeping up my chest and demanded to be released. It stood right inside my heart and pounded loudly for me to hear. I thought, "Okay, universe, I get it, another lesson, but do I have any stamina left?!" I systematically destroyed all that I had known, rejecting old habits, people and situations that no longer served me. In this process, being held safely by a brilliant therapist and several coaches, I discovered some harsh realities about my life and upbringing. I allowed the memories to surface, felt them deeply and then burned them down to the ground. I re-wrote the narrative I was telling myself, in a safe space. I was in the throes of reinvention, and there was no stopping me. Not even I could stop myself if I wanted to.

At the same time, I was promoted at my new job and started my certification in Health Coaching. I was finally being recognized for my unique skills, validated in my work and listening to my intuition and desires! Despite this progress, I continued to binge, unable to stop, officially "face down in the food," still embracing my Phoenix process. I couldn't stop and I was gaining weight. The feared floodgates had opened, and my worst nightmare was becoming a reality.

But at the same time, I was coming alive in new ways. I discovered that I was not sure how to sit with the discomfort of being okay in some areas of my life and didn't know why I wasn't okay with being okay. What I realized was that all I had known in my life until then was chaos and turmoil. The feeling of pleasure was foreign. The feelings of contentedness were scary and felt unattainable.

A theme in my life appeared: as soon as I started feeling okay, I did things to sabotage myself. I couldn't handle being thin and "showing myself" to the world, and I couldn't handle being "fat" either. Even though I desperately wanted to be seen, I wanted to hide simultaneously. My brain told me things like "It's ok to let go, you are safe now," immediately followed by "NO, don't let go, eat food instead, it is your only safety." I felt like I was in the clothes dryer being bounced around with no footing. "Success" felt unfamiliar to my brain and therefore unsafe. I was trying to change the script and heal. My brain wanted to do the opposite and keep me safe with its old destructive methods, trying to override my new habits of wellness with old patterns that worked before. My brain wanted to stay where it had been lodged all its life, safely nestled up for so long, crumpled up in a comfy cozy fetal position wreaking havoc on my life and body.

What got me from there, a place of just beginning to heal, to here—a place of consistent healing and growth? The answer is willingness. I developed a willingness to learn, a willingness to grow, and a willingness to shed all that came before. A willingness to put myself on the cross again and this time, change everything about the way I viewed the world. I had to shed the old and make space for shiny new things. I learned through coaching and self-discovery that it is my job to hack the system called my brain. It is my job to unveil the old narratives that tell me I can't, and convert them into "How can I?" I learned that just because someone tells me I should do something doesn't mean it's right for *me*. I slowly learned how to organically listen to my body and intuition. I learned that during those conflicting moments, when heart and brain felt misaligned, that my intuition was talking. Learning to hear my intuition felt like learning how to walk or ride a bike. Like something I should have already known and that I missed out on. I learned I can have both and more and even weigh the options before I decide.

Why don't people do this more often? Because it's *hard*. It's really, really hard and it takes practice like building your muscles at the gym. You have to work out to build muscle. It's way easier to stay in victimhood and be consumed by the past. It's comfy there, where everything is predictable and seemingly "safe," where all is well. My brain thought that its old default behaviors, like binging and risky behavior, were safe. After all, those methods worked for 20 years. But I had to tell it otherwise.

I now have an entire team dedicated to *me*. I had to realize that I am *worth* investing in a team, just for *me*. I have guides, coaches, therapists, mentors, friends and great doctors who listen. I choose my tribe, using great care and discernment on who gets to be on the inside. Today, in this new me, with newly uploaded software, I refuse to entertain anyone who will decrease my bandwidth and strain my network. My bandwidth is a precious commodity, made up of billions of cells, hundreds of hours of self-work, discovery and practice. I have earned the right to be selective with my sacred project.

I am deeply grateful for my mentors, coaches, angels, and love lenders. At one point or another they were all scared for my life and weathered the storm *with* me, by my side. Not in judgment, not in front of me, but by my side. Without a strong support system, I would not have made it this far, this story wouldn't have been written and they would be visiting me at my headstone. Because of the supports in my life, I have developed a deep sense that I am going to be okay after all, and that I don't have to do it alone.

Health coaching was also a pivotal step in my own personal healing. I took big, bold action, went back to school, against all my "schooling" fears, got certified in Health and Life Coaching and even went on to advanced courses to become a Master Coach! Now, I help people who are stuck like I was. People in burnout, overweight, struggling with mental health instability, addiction, and disordered eating patterns. People who are paralyzed, scared and see no way out. I hold space for my clients' to come undone. I am a healer, a vessel for transformation and a fierce advocate for self love. I believe intensely that my clients can have what they desire, uncover the layers of Kevlar wrapped around their intuition and heart and start to see their worth.

Instead of shielding others from my true self and essence, I walk in full beaming light spilling on to the world. I am my unique brand of me, unapologetically. I no longer feel like I have to protect the world from my magic, empathy and essence. I no longer fear that I am "too much" or "too dramatic" for anyone. I am no longer afraid of myself. I feel gratitude for the painful lessons that have transcended me into my full and thriving true self. I forgive my light thieves, because I understand that my light is so bright that it is in high demand in this hurting world. I was given a gift of light and hope that people wanted to steal for themselves. I understand that hurt people hurt people and I understand the cyclical and repetitious compulsion of perpetrators, even if it makes others cringe. To the light thieves: my personal message to you is that you find the serenity and balance that you are seeking, from within, not in thievery.

I believe in the power of story, transparency, and the force of personal power. I believe that if I share my story that I will help to ignite the same fire and fight in someone else reading this who is suffering, mouth full and dripping with chocolate, heart aching with insecurity. I want this story to reach the reader who contemplated committing suicide an hour ago while driving in the car, wondering why they are still choosing to live this painful life. I want this to help the single mother who's working two jobs to pay the heating bill not knowing how she will go on. I want to help the man who is afraid of his tremendous power and wants to stop hiding. I want the girl who is being bullied in silence to read this and know that her story matters. I want the domestic violence survivor to read this and know that their body and opinion matters, even when they are told it doesn't. I want the felon reading this to know that they too are worth the effort. I want the sweet empath reading this to know that they are not *too* anything, not a black sheep and not too sensitive. *You* are exactly what you are meant to be in all your glory, and you are on purpose.

You are your unique brand of you, embrace your brand. You are worthy and you are not alone. You can borrow *my* faith until you have yours back. I had to borrow the faith of others for years, hanging on by a thread. It was those cumulative moments and shards of thread that eventually manifested into to a string, that lead to a swatch, that lead to a blanket that lead to my new thriving life.

I am still growing and evolving every day, regardless of my diagnoses or current relationship with food. Not every day is full of sparkles and rainbows, so, I call in reinforcements when I need them. I work on graciously receiving gifts and work on asking for help. Today, I am a new person, in new glowing skin, with a new spirit and experiencing my first shot at what I call *real* life. I see the past memories as fragments of my tattered and beautiful life. The glitter of my life, delightfully pink, shiny and feminine, catching the golden rays of the sunlight just right, blanketing my new life with a glowing film of experience, pain, depth and passion. I consider this the first time I have lived life, ever, not a second chance at life, but my first ever.

To those of you who find solace in this story, resonate with any of its parts, or hate it completely and stopped reading at page two, please consider coaching, therapy or some other form of support to help you gain some strength and clarity. And if you never seek out support, know that I hold space for your healing and relief. Suffering in silence is not necessary or sustainable. Turning in on yourself is not productive if you are seeking an upgraded version of your life. Although it might feel like hiding is keeping you safe, it will forever remain fruitless, keeping you in the same loop of desperation.

If you want more for yourself and want to be all-in with your own life, take one small step forward. Little actions can get big results. As soon as I said yes to myself and shifted my energy, an entire world of possibility unfolded for me. It was always there waiting to unfold, I just needed to take baby steps to begin to see it. I am now a successful life and health coach, with loved ones around me, intact and walking in my truth. I still have bad days, they're just much less frequent.

I am no longer broken; I am awake and thriving. My work is not done and never will be. If my work is done, then I am no longer growing. If I am no longer growing, I am no longer feeling. If I am no longer feeling, I am no longer truly living. I have learned that the beauty is in the dance, in the skillful teeter-totter that we call balance. The magic is not in the box of cookies, the bottle of pills or the end of a revolver. The magic is in the dance.

I wish you abundant wellness, clarity and good health and leave you with this word, UBUNTU: "The belief in a universal bond of sharing that connects all humanity."

NOTE: (Please see the resource section in the back of this book for contact information for immediate professional support).

STEPS TO TRUE INNER HAPPINESS

By: Teresa Greco

There was something about turning 40-years-old that made me stop in my tracks and ask myself some pretty important questions—perhaps what one might even consider life-altering questions. I have heard people use the phrase "mid-life crisis" when they reach 40 years of life and suddenly decide to make significant changes in their life. Turning 40 had me asking myself the all-important questions: "Where is my life going?", "Am I happy in the life I am living?", "Can I imagine myself living the same life for another 40 years?", "Is there more to life than just this?" And most notably, there was the question, "Am I living my life's true purpose and full potential here on Earth?" This last question had me reflecting about whether I was being myself and using all the gifts God had given me to make a difference in the world. Was I making a positive difference, day in and day out? I have been blessed with a healthy body and a healthy mind and was I using these blessings to their fullest potential, or could I be doing more? Internally I felt that something was missing and that I was destined for more, but what?

I'll never forget the day I met a dear friend of mine for lunch at a restaurant that was convenient for the both of us to get to. Jennifer arrived with her two-year-old in tow. I, on the other hand, was by myself because my two children, who were older than Jennifer's, were in Montessori school during the day. As Jennifer settled her son into the restaurant highchair, we both ordered a cup of coffee to start. The restaurant was rumbling with action. Most of the tables were occupied with patrons and the wait staff bustled around, cleaning tables and bringing people their food. The smell of fresh fruit and waffles filled the air from the nearby open kitchen. Not sure what to order at first, I decided on an omelet with a side of hash browns and Jennifer ordered the same.

Jennifer and I had been friends since elementary school. If anyone knew me well, it was Jennifer. It didn't take her long to sense that something was amiss with me that day. My usual positive energy and bubbly personality had been replaced with a sullen expression on my face, as I held the hot coffee mug in both hands, my head and eyes lowered. Like best friends do, Jennifer got right down to it and asked me if everything was okay. With the feeling of safety I always felt in her presence, I divulged a truth that no one, not even my husband, knew I felt. As hot tears began to stream down my face, I murmured, "My life is not my own." This was one of the hardest statements I had ever said to myself, let alone aloud to another. I had admitted audibly something I had been feeling internally for a long time but that felt selfish to express aloud. I had indeed lost myself in my everyday responsibilities that filled my time.

Jennifer responded to my heartfelt statement with a very matter of fact comment, as she spooned cereal into her son's mouth. "Teresa, of course you feel like that. You have two small kids at home. You're managing your house, your work, your studies. It's hard for you to have time for yourself."

It was evident by Jennifer's response that she had missed the gravity of what these words meant to me and the deep despondency I felt throughout every inch of my body. The issue was not so much about having time for myself as it was about how I was living my day to day. Was I living my life according to Teresa, or was I living my day to day according to what everyone else expected me to do? Was I being my true self or was I trying to live up to external expectations set out for me by my family, friends, religion, culture, and society? It was then that I realized it was the latter. There was a clarity in that moment of vocalization that wasn't there a minute before. Goosebumps covered my body while an immense sadness filled my heart. I now knew I had somehow lost myself in the living of my life.

At the time, my life was busy. But I told myself, wasn't everybody's? Like many women my age, most of my time was consumed with being a mother and growing up my two children. Being a mother is the greatest, hardest, and most rewarding blessing in the world. I was having a co-habiting relationship with my husband. Both of us were engrossed in our own day-to-day responsibilities, which left little time and energy to focus on ourselves and our relationship. I was teaching part-time at a private school. Teaching fulfilled me on many levels; I have always felt that being a teacher is my destined profession and an extension of myself. I was also studying at a university because I love learning new things and using my newfound knowledge to help others. I was maintaining a household on my own (cooking, cleaning, laundry, and so on) while my husband was working selflessly to support our family. Lastly, any remaining time consisted of my efforts to maintain my health, energy, positivity, and sanity by going to the gym regularly and reading books that nourished me spiritually.

So, with all this going on, why did I still feel so empty and incomplete? Questions continued to resound in my head, "Was there more to my life than this?", "If I was living the life God gave me to its fullest potential, why do I feel so incomplete inside?", "Maybe if I make a grander difference in the world, I'll feel more fulfilled internally?" I didn't know the answers to these questions yet. All I knew was that something was missing.

But how did all this doubt and insecurity happen within me? Over the years of growing up in a traditional Italian household, with two parents and three sisters, how did I forget who I was as a little girl and become a 40-year-old woman who felt incomplete and not who she was meant to be in this life? How did I get to 40, with all the blessings you could ever need, and still feel imperfect? How does someone who, on the outside, appears to have everything she desires, still feel as though something is lacking? In order to answer these questions, I needed to deconstruct the belief system I had adopted for my life. I needed to realize that I couldn't continue on trying to be the perfect daughter, wife, mother, or whoever I needed to be for everyone else while not respecting my own desires and opinions.

As the eldest daughter in a nuclear family, I was brought up to believe certain things about being a "good woman." Ingrained within me by my family, culture, society, and religion were some traditional beliefs and expectations. For example, the "good mom" brought her kids to play groups, read to them every day, only allowed them to watch educational videos, and fed them homemade food. The "good mom" also stayed home with her kids and didn't put them in daycare. The "good wife" would have dinner ready every day when her husband came home, have clean clothes ready for him to wear, and sent him to work with a lunch in a paper bag. The "good daughter" was one who called her mom every day, who wore enough makeup but not too much makeup, who dressed up nicely but not too nicely because "Who are you trying to impress? You already have a husband," she would say to me. And as you probably know, many mothers aren't subtle about letting you know what they think. In trying to please everyone else, I wasn't pleasing myself or respecting my own personal beliefs. This would often leave me feeling resentful, voiceless, offended, and upset.

Through the adoption of the practices and beliefs I outline in this chapter, I was able to find not just my voice, but *myself*. And in finding myself, I found the happiness I was lacking. I finally understood my feeling of "something is missing," or "there must be something more than just this" when that space inside of me was filled by true inner happiness. It was about reaching that point where I no longer had to look outside myself for "things" that will make you happy. There was no void to fill with "toys" (i.e., designer clothes or hand-bags, luxury cars, a huge home, frequent vacations, flashy friends or social media followers). I realized that once I was filled with inner happiness, I no longer desired to be filled by the external things that society told me I needed to obtain to be happy. The desire to have the perfect fairy tale relation-ship, the next best "you gotta have this" item, or the feeling of "having to keep up with the Joneses" in order to feel happy and complete didn't exist anymore. There was also no looking for the approval of others to validate me as a person. The desire to be the "perfect" mother, daughter, daughter-in-law, sister, etc., etc. wasn't necessary when I started to live as my authentic self. Living authentically meant that I was no lon-ger searching for ways to make other people happy with my actions. I was now able to know that when I do something in my own unique way and I am 110% loving in my actions and my intentions, then it doesn't matter whether anyone else approves or disapproves. I am no longer interested in know-ing about the opinions of others to validate me as a person. Instead I have learned to use and trust my intuition to guide me and to know whether I am approaching my life in a way that reflects who I am as a person.

When I began to follow the steps below, something else happened that I didn't expect—I discovered some-thing I didn't know I lacked until I found it: self-love. When I began feeling love for myself, I started feeling happier and more fulfilled. I realized I was sabotaging myself as well, with the negative opinions of myself repeating themselves in my head.

Your ego is the conditioned part of yourself—the part that becomes molded by things external to you: your family and friends, culture, religion, and society. And the ego's voice is often negative because it reflects our fear-based and judgmental culture we live in. Over time, these external factors and opinions became ingrained beliefs in me and my ego's voice was what I heard the loudest. My ego's voice told me, "You need to improve." "You need to be skinnier and prettier." "You need to be the perfect wife, daughter/in-law, mother, sister, friend, and employee." "You need someone to complete you because if you're alone, you are less than whole." "You need to have more university degrees and more work experience, because as a woman you need options." It went on and on. The desire to improve, do more, and be better than who I was became the Teresa who felt incomplete, insufficient, imperfect, and less than whole. It seemed as though the more I tried to achieve these goals, the more I failed at them. Actually, it felt like all anybody ever did was complain about how I was falling short of their expectations. Adopting the following practices allowed me to rewrite the negative voices in my head, the voices of my ego, with positive thoughts that serve me and reflect my loving, inner-spirit.

Turning 40 was my reason to start making changes in my life because I couldn't continue living according to everyone else's expectations. It was my reason to start living my life on my terms. Turning 40 was my wake-up call to reclaim my life and start living my life authentically by honoring and respecting myself first. My story is about how I began to discover who I was meant to be in this lifetime and to *uncover* my spirit's purpose. I was a gem but unpolished. The changes I made allowed me to uncover the iridescent diamond beneath the blurred and rough facade. This chapter is about how I found self-love, true and genuine inner-happiness, and some of the steps I took that led me there.

STEP 1: IT ALL BEGAN WITH MEDITATION

From as young as I can remember, I always believed in and felt connected to something greater than just this human existence. I have had different experiences when Spirit, Source, God, the Universe, or whatever term you choose to use, showed its existence to me. There were unquestionable events that illustrated to me that God exists and there is more than just the physical which we take in with our senses. Over the years, I came to believe that my spirit is inside of me and through prayer I could connect to that part of myself. Through prayer, I could also communicate with God, who was outside of me. As a Roman Catholic, I was taught that God existed in Heaven and Jesus existed in the tabernacle in my church (metaphorically speaking). Because God was external to me, I needed to go to church to be with him or go to my priest, who would communicate with God for me. There was something about this ideology that never jived with me. It seemed odd that I needed a mediator to speak with the Source who had created me.

In prayer I repeatedly asked God for guidance. For years I asked God to help me to hear him better, but no signs or inclinations seemed to present themselves. Feeling as though I had reached a point where I needed some direction as to how I was going to make this happen, I decided to see a medium. A highly recommended medium was invited to do multiple readings for a few people at my friend's house. During my session, which took place in the basement of her home, I sat opposite the medium on a velvet yellow couch. After expressing my interest in being able to hear and communicate more with God, the medium shared Spirit's message with me, which was to meditate. Meditate, I queried? What did I know about meditation?

I didn't know where to begin. But luckily for me, there was a meditation centre close by my home and my spiritual mentors (as I like to call them) helped me to get started. If you are like me, where the idea of meditation sounds daunting and you're also not sure where or how to begin, seeking out a meditation centre or meditation circle is an awesome way to get started. They will guide you through what to do with your body and how to settle your mind to help get the process started. I have also used guided meditations on YouTube in the comfort and privacy of my own home. Guided meditations are particularly helpful because they give you something to focus on and follow in your mind. The guide will instruct you to relax specific muscles in your body until they are comfortable and will then lead you through mental images and visualizations. You can even choose from guided meditations based on different themes such as letting go, sleep meditations, weight loss, and forgiveness.

The meditation centre I attend one evening a month takes place in the home of my spiritual mentors. It is an older home with original wood floors, adorned with antique furniture in small living spaces. When you enter, you are often greeted and warmly embraced by the proprietors. You are also struck by the smell of the smoke of white sage, which is always burned prior to us arriving (a practice known as smudging). The air is filled with a distinctly beautiful herbaceous and woodsy scent, intended to cleanse you of any negative energy you might be carrying with you from the stresses of the day. I make my way to the living room where the circle is held, often surrounded by other welcoming and smiling guests who had already found a spot to sit down. I always choose a seat on the soft, white sofa. We are encircled by lit candles, which creates a warm ambiance in the room. In the center of the room is a coffee table, which has more illuminated candles and several boxes of oracle cards displayed. Our time together always begins with my mentors at the front of the circle, sitting in vintage wingback chairs, welcoming the group and setting our intentions for the evening. We then begin our first meditation.

My first couple meditations at the centre were intense. The very first time, just like all the subsequent times, I was instructed to close my eyes, sit upright with my arms and legs uncrossed and palms facing upward. Soft music with the sounds of nature began to fall upon my ears. One of my mentors then began to guide the meditation with instructions to visualize our chakra centers and their respective colours in different areas of our body. Following her directions (as I didn't know much about chakra centers at the time), I soon found my body melting away as my mind became focused and immersed in the light in my mind's eye. The physical space I was in dissipated, and the weight-lessness and absence of my physical body felt unnerving, like nothing I had ever experienced before. My mind was being consumed by the white light beaming down from above on what seemed like the essence of my being. My energy, my spirit, was then joined by an energy more pow-erful and loving than my own. I could feel my spirit in the company of a higher power. It was in that moment that I knew I was not alone. I felt my spirit surrounded by other energies. The energies are filled with so much love that at first, it felt overwhelming. I had never felt the potency of a love so unconditional and without judgment. The immense love I felt in that dimension, if I can call it that, took me aback, brought tears to my eyes, and I had trouble catching my breath. I reached for the tissue box as I was then quietly sobbing. I had this innate feeling as though I had come home to where I came from and had finally connected with God, my creator. I was also able to connect with my spirit, the infinite and immortal part of myself. Through meditation I was and still am reminded of who I really am, love and light. The greatness, wholeness, and awesomeness of who I really am is invariably felt in that dimension.

It was through meditation that I discovered I can com-municate directly with God without a mediator! Imagine that! God wasn't outside of me at Church; God is a part of me and I a part of God. Through meditation I connect with this infinite part of myself, which is the energy that lives forever and returns to God when my shell (my physical body) dies. This energy is pure, unconditional love. The realization that I can connect with my true self and be enveloped by God in that dimension at any time through meditation gives me a feeling of security and refuge. If you ever feel alone and unnoticed, you can experience this immense love that is available for you to tap into whenever you mediate. God's love is unconditional, always there, and ready to swaddle you just as you are.

When meditating, you may leave time and space and find yourself in the NOW, which is God's Moment. We abandon time and therefore abandon the physical Universe that constricts our understanding of where our spirit comes from and limits our existence to just the physical realm. You know you are in the NOW when you no longer feel your body or your physical surroundings. It is like escaping the present and moving into a space where the physical no longer exists or even matters. Anything you might have been feeling before entering that moment with God is gone. Any frustration, anger, inadequacies, resentment, or stress wash away. Any skeletons from your past, "monkeys on your back," or past mistakes instantly dissolve as you feel only love on the other side. Knowing that I can escape the trivialities of my physical world and come home to where my spirit resides and be blanketed with unconditional love gives me the strength to love and forgive myself and others more in my everyday life.

When I finally experienced the love always present for me when meditating, I realized that I didn't feel this love for myself on a day to day basis. I had not been loving myself my whole life. There were days I liked myself a little more than others, but I definitely didn't love myself completely as I should have. If anything, I had been cruel and demeaning to myself. Being my worse critic instead of my best cheerleader. I tore myself down every day with belittling comments and disparaging judgments. I wasn't thin enough. Or smart enough. Or beautiful enough. Or kind enough. Or giving enough. The truth was I felt like this because I was disconnected from Source energy, and thus disconnected from the unconditional love that was inside of me the whole time. I had forgotten where I, my spirit, came from. And finally, I awoke to myself, the infinite energy that fuels my personality every day.

In God's Moment, you are more than just your body, your accomplishments, your possessions, and your titles or labels. You realize that you are pure energy, an energy that is limitless and abundant. You are whole and perfect just as you are, each of us in our own unique way. The desire to perfect and improve ourselves every day is not necessary. We already are perfect. Our earthly task is to rediscover our spiritual perfection and allow it to embrace us in our everyday lives. When we let go of time and space and enter into God's Moment through the act of meditation, our perfect self lives there. And it is there where we are reminded of who we really are. When you tap into the "infinite field of potentiality" (Pat Grout's word for Source energy), you begin to recognize that "we are not human beings having a spiritual experience. We are spiritual beings having a human experience." (Pierre Teilhard de Chardin). I try to meditate often because we all need reminding of who we are and where we actually came from. Reminding ourselves of this is crucial when our physical world tears us down and fears us out of living our full potential and our destined selves. I know when I need to meditate because I start to revert back to my old patterns of negative self-talk. There is a feeling of malaise and my level of positive energy is low. If people or situations around me have been upsetting and are drawing on my energy, I know it is time for me to meditate, recharge, and connect with my inner spirit and with God.

I can also attest to the feeling of not wanting to come back to Earth when you are in God's Moment because it feels so good when you are there. For me, there's a weightlessness and a brightness that feels so euphoric it is hard to come back to the physical world. But as our spirit came to Earth to have this Earthly experience, we slowly open our eyes and return to our physical bodies. Having been reminded however of who we are in meditation, our spirit is re-energized and we are more adept at tackling our physical world with more love and forgiveness for ourselves and for others. Becoming attuned to this Universal Energy Source through meditation has only strengthened my relationship with myself and with God and I experience the Universe's presence in my life every day. I experience small miracles each day as the Universe's way of saying, "I love you and we are always with you." Knowing I am never alone and loved unconditionally, just as I am, has helped me to embrace who I am and remember to love and honor myself every day.

STEP 2: LETTING GO OF THE FEAR AND WORRY OF BEING ME

When I consciously choose happiness over feelings of fear and worry, my life flows with ease. We live in a fear-based society. We are surrounded by circumstances, events, and information that induce feelings of fear. We also feel fear about letting people see our true selves and for fear of rejection, we live lives very differently from who we were meant to be. I want to address the fear that prevents us from living our true selves. This is a fear I needed to wake up to that I wasn't aware of until I began to love myself more. It's a fear we develop as we get older and become more aware of how other people see us, feel about us, and judge us.

As young children, we live fearlessly, exploring the world with awe and excitement. However, as we get older, we become more self-aware and with that awareness we develop our self-image, self-concept, and self-consciousness. My earliest recollections of developing self-awareness came via comments made by people around me (family, friends, doctors, teachers and classmates). The negative comments that stung the most were those that when I heard them, stuck to me with Crazy Glue. These comments led to beliefs about myself that ultimately limited my ability to live my life to its fullest potential and impacted the love I felt for myself. Negative comments about my weight, my intellect, my athletic abilities, and my physical body all had a damaging effect on how I saw myself. Comments such as these cut deeply, made me want to break down and cry (but I resisted the tears) and have weighed me down my whole life. At school, teachers and classmates blurted malicious comments such as, "You're fat." "You're dumb." "I can't believe you got an A." "You're too fat to run fast." "You're too fat to climb those ropes." "You get As?"

"You're smart enough for that?" "You're too heavy."

Family and friends senselessly declared, "You weigh too much for your age." "You look fat in those jeans." "You should watch what you eat." "You're eating too much."

Co-workers verbalized demeaning statements such as "Your legs are fat." "Your legs are too big." "Your nose is big." With enough repetition, I internalized those comments and they soon became my own. They became a part of what I said to myself inside my mind every time I looked in the mirror, tried something on, played a sport, or pursued an academic interest. In my mind I was the fat, really tall girl with big legs who was kinda dumb and couldn't do sports because she was fat and slow. I became my worst critic. I punished myself with the same harsh criticisms, day in and day out. These thoughts about myself aided in my insecurities. I became insecure about how I looked, what I said, and how I behaved.

Growing up in a culture where everyone has an opinion and constantly judges others negatively, it makes sense that one would judge themselves and compare themselves to a societal standard of beauty and successfulness. And in my mind, I never seemed to measure up to that societal standard. My insecurities contributed to fears I had about my appearance, my abilities, what I could do and achieve, and perhaps even what I was worthy of. And when I was succeeding or feeling good about myself and my accomplishments, I played it small. Playing it small meant I didn't share my successes and accomplishments, or my dreams and aspirations with others. I didn't share these things for fear of being judged as "being better than" or "who do you think you are" or "how did *you* achieve that?" To avoid the criticism or belittling, I kept even the positive things about myself to myself.

I now realize that playing it small and living the "Small Teresa" was letting fear control my life. Fearing what people will say and think of me affects how I perceive myself, my self-worth, my self-esteem, and my abilities. It affects how I see myself on the inside and on the outside in the mirror. It affects the voice in my head and the words I say to myself. Becoming cognitive of this fear and how it is affecting my life has allowed me to change the voice. We know words have power. Positive words can motivate, inspire, give courage and strength, encourage the pursuing of our dreams, raise expectations, share love (kindness, and joy), and ultimately transform lives. I have replaced the limiting beliefs about myself with positive, uplifting, and encouraging statements. I have rewritten the comments of my childhood with positive affirmations which I practice daily.

We also know that words can have a negative and even detrimental effect on us. Negative words can lower our self-esteem, demean, hurt, damage, and instill self-doubt. Negative self-talk can create our own glass ceiling and keep us from reaching our full potential. Because words influence our thoughts, and our thoughts determine our actions, and our actions determine our experiences, we want to make sure our words are positive and self-loving.

Using daily positive affirmations is a key to self-love. Affirmations are a proven way to change our thoughts, which in turn changes our world. Dr. Wayne Dyer even entitled a book on our ability to *Change your thoughts, Change your life*. Dr. Joseph Dispenza, author of *Physics, the Brain and Your Reality*, speaks of the science that has found that saying positive affirmations works to rewire the brain by creating new neural pathways and rewriting the thoughts from negative to positive in our subconscious mind. By repeating positive statements about ourselves, neuroscience has proven that our brain begins to believe the new statements and even elicits positive physical changes in the body such as reducing stress, reducing blood pressure and improving one's sleep. I use affirmations daily but especially in moments when I feel I need to affirm who I am or who I want to be. The impact of affirming myself came with the use of the I AM affirmation. The I AM affirmation was given to us by Jesus in his use of the words in his own statements such as: "I AM the resurrection and the life," "I AM the Light of the world," and "I AM the Way, the Truth and the Life" (John 14:6). Using the words I AM allows us to connect to our higher selves and therefore to God. What that means is that if you use the words I AM before positive statements about yourself, you are harnessing the power of God to change you, your life, and to manifest your desires. Whatever follows the words "I AM" starts the creation of those words. Stating the goal from the end and affirming it with your thoughts, emotions and words sets the Universe into motion to make things happen for you. I have used the following I AM statements to affirm myself and the person I want to be: "I AM smart. I AM intelligent. I AM friendly. I AM a team player. I AM the best person for this job." Notice I am not using the words "I hope to be" or "I want to be." I am using the phrase I AM as it already exists. I am intelligent *now*. I am a team player *now*. There are times when old habits slip in and I begin to feel less confident about myself and how I look. It is during these times that I affirm myself using these statements: "I AM beautiful. I AM a good person. I AM generous. I AM an amazing mother. I AM healthy. I AM abundant. I AM loved and cared for. I AM love. I AM peace." It is through the use of these positive affirmations that I have learned to love, honour, and respect myself.

I ask you to reflect on yourself and the voice in your head. Ask yourself this question and honestly evaluate if the people around you know the real you. Are you living your authentic self every day? Has fear forced you to live your "small self?" The "big self" resides within us and believes we are capable of anything we set our minds to, regardless of whether others approve or believe we can achieve it. The "big self" has our deepest desires, wishes, dreams, and aspirations for our life. I believe the "big self" is our spirit, who knows what we are capable of and what goals and aspirations we had for ourselves before coming down here to Earth. My "big self" wants to write, do motivational speaking, and help change the world for the better, one person at a time. My "big self" knows the gifts I have been blessed with and asks me to share those gifts with the world every day. Your "big self" could be the voice you are stuffing down or placing on mute, just as I did my whole life. You'll recognize it as the things you want to do or try but let fear get in the way. Your spirit calls out to try new things or to pursue an inner wish or desire, but you let fear and worry talk you out of it.

Fear is the voice that rationalizes you out of pursuing those desires and goals. Ask yourself, is fear or worry preventing you from going to the next level (i.e., getting that promotion at work) because you're afraid of failing or think you're not capable enough? Is fear preventing you from travelling outside of the country because you're afraid of flying or afraid of what could happen to you outside your familiar surroundings? Are you afraid of changing jobs, where you live, who your friends are, who your partner is because the unknown could be worse? But what if it wasn't? What if what your spirit has planned for you is even better than where you are now? What if what was in store for you was even bigger and greater than what you have now? What if you were happier on your own than in a relationship that brought you down instead of lifted you up? What if not hanging out with these "friends" made room or made time for you to meet new people, perhaps people who were more like you? What if taking that flight allowed you to experience new things, things you could never have imagined in your wildest dreams? What if you decided to be more "you" today? What would that look like for you?

When I began loving myself more, I also began listening to and believing that internal voice within me, the voice of my spirit. My spirit's voice tells me "I can do it," "I can achieve it," "You are beautiful just as you are," "You are perfect just as you are," "You are equal to others," and "You have what it takes to achieve your highest wishes, dreams, and aspirations for yourself." I have replaced the voices of the past with my spirit's voice of encouragement, cheer, and praise. Believing my inner spirit's voice gives me the courage and strength to follow and pursue its wishes and desires. I no longer let the voices of fear and worry have a command over my life and limit what I can do or achieve. I choose to not care about what others think about me and my pursuits. I no longer seek the approval of others to know if who I am or what I am doing is acceptable or good enough. I don't ask those around me what they think about things I am doing or want to do. I don't ask their opinion about what I wear, how I prepare myself, or projects I am working on. I let that inner voice guide me instead. I use my internal barometer to let me know if what I am doing is right and just, and if it reflects the real and authentic me. Your internal barometer will give you either positive or negative feelings about something. You'll know if you listen carefully enough to it. Use your intuition to guide you. If your intuition says it feels good and it is right thing to do, then give it a try. Believe me, when you've done something that isn't reflective of your spirit, it feels lousy and you'll know you probably haven't acted out of love with your thoughts, words, and actions.

Letting go of the need to please others by trying to meet their expectations of their ideal and perfect mother, wife, daughter, etc. has opened up space for the true inner me to shine through and to live life according to my own spirit's desires and wishes. Trusting in myself and my inner spirit's voice has allowed me to start living my "big self" and not let fear and worry prevent me from living my true and authentic self every day.

STEP 3: CHOOSING A LIFE OF HAPPINESS AND PASSION

Have you ever woken up and thought to yourself, "Today is a brand-new day, with a fresh new start!" Each day is a new day when you can *choose* to leave your past in the past and choose to start new and fresh again today. Notice the word "choose." It is exactly that, a choice. We can choose what our thoughts will be today. *We can choose to be happy today* by consciously saying "Stop!" to the old thoughts that no longer serve us. When I have thoughts from the past come into my mind that I no longer want to think about or dwell on, I deliberately say "Stop!" This is a strategy I practice often—literally saying "Stop" to negative past experiences or discouraging patterns of self-talk and I intentionally replace those thoughts by choosing new ones that I want to have instead, which serve me in a positive way. I choose to leave the negative events from my past exactly there, in the past.

Each morning is like a reset button that allows you to make new choices for a life that serves the inner you, your spirit. We can choose new thoughts that elicit feelings of happiness within us. What happy thoughts do I want to have? Thoughts of gratitude and joy. Thoughts of things, places and people which bring me happiness when I think about them. When I open my eyes each morning and I have been blessed to live one more day, I consciously decide to live it as if it was my last. Life is too short to be stuck in the past or down in the trenches; it is a very great gift and fragile as a flower.

Recognize the blessings that lie before you and give thanks for them—simple things like the bed you were able to sleep in, the legs that can take you into the washroom to begin getting ready for the day, or the car you have that takes you to work with ease and comfort. I have a gratitude practice where every morning (soon after I awake) and every evening (just before falling asleep) I give thanks for all the blessings in my life. This starts each day with a positive tone and when practiced at night, takes my blessings into my subconscious mind and invites more of these same blessings to come into my future.

Your new day does not need to be like yesterday either. What changes can you make so that today can be just a little different than yesterday? We are creatures of habit. Our body lives 96% of its day from the subconscious; where we follow the same routine we did yesterday and probably the day before that and the day before that one. Sure, it's easy. Sure, it's comforting. But what happens when you look back at the last 35, 25 or 10 years of your life and say, "Where did it all go?" "What did I do over all these years that was memorable, that was enjoyable?" Have you been living only to work or working to "live"?

Dr. Joseph Dispenza, in the book *Breaking the Habit of Being Yourself*, states we have 60,000 to 70,000 thoughts a day and 90% of those thoughts are the same as yesterday's. It is not a wonder, then, that many of us wake up morning after morning and do the same things. We wake up, get to work (maybe even at a job we hate and/or work with people we dislike), return home, eat, watch TV, go to sleep and do the same thing all over again tomorrow, without even realizing that our life is passing us by, that we're getting older, and that there is more to life than the rat race. You may begin wondering, "Is this what life is all about?" Some people might be caught in the endless cycle of working to pay for a house that is beyond their means, buying clothes and cars beyond their budget, trying to keep up with the Joneses, all while going to a job that isn't their passion to pay for the things that have them living beyond their means.

Each one of us is here to live our passion, to pursue our interests, and to do what ignites a fire inside of us. We're all different in this way. I love it when I meet someone who says while working at their craft, "This is my passion," or "This is my calling," or "This is my baby" (meaning a project or venture they're working on). Are you living your passion every day? Are you doing what excites and energizes you? Do you have a job that you love so much it never feels like work to you and Monday isn't the worst day of the week? We all have a choice. Find what your passion is and find ways to make your passion your career. Feel what makes you happy when you do it. Do what feels effortless and doesn't feel like work when you do it. It could be what you always think about when your thoughts begin to wander. It could also be what you repeatedly dream about. Life is too short to live most of your waking hours at a job you dislike or makes you sick to the point you need to medicate yourself to feel less stressed or less depressed, and then to commute hours to and from a job that doesn't fulfill you in any way.

We are here to spread God's love to others and to make a difference in whatever way we can. We do this quite simply by doing what makes us happy, because when we are happy, those around us are happy too. We do this by being our authentic selves and letting the light inside of us shine through. If we follow the signs from the Universe and listen to that inner voice, we will be guided towards where we need to be and do what we need to be doing to spread God's light and love with the world.

Making tough decisions (like leaving a stressful and toxic job for one that earns less money) and taking a leap of faith (that our next phase will be better) can bring us closer to living the life we were really meant to live here on Earth. Don't you want to find out what that life is? You had a pre-determined path before you came down here to Earth and when we stick to our path, there's a flow and ease to our life. You might even say you're living a Heaven on Earth. However, if your new day feels more like a Hell on Earth, then it is possible that you have strayed so far away from your original and predestined path and now you feel more miserable than you do happy.

So ask yourself, "If this were my last day on Earth, what would I want it to be like?" Are you making choices that will bring you closer to living a Heaven on Earth? Take the necessary steps that will bring you closer to living a life where you spread God's light and love with others by just being yourself and by doing what makes you feel truly and genuinely happy inside!

It takes great strength, courage, and honor (honoring thyself) to live life according to you! I have managed to find these traits inside of me, although I did need to dig deep and learn lessons along the way (orchestrated by the Universe) to discover a level of strength and courage I didn't know I had in me to reclaim *my* life—my life according to Teresa and not according to anyone else. I have had to learn to let go of people's perceptions, opinions, and judgments of me and understand that ultimately, it is not my issue if they have a problem with my actions and/or choices. It is in these moments of contrast that you learn or realize who really loves you and who truly is a friend. Those are the people who will stick by you even when you are making a choice they wouldn't make for themselves. Life is too short to have superficial relationships anyway, I say. By this age, I want to have authentic friendships and real relationships with people around me. I want to be surrounded by people who love me, who feel that I bring value to their lives, and who want to be by me sincerely. I'd rather be by myself if I have to BE someone else just to be to loved, liked, or in the company of others. Finding such people (those who are similar to us) can be difficult, but if we stay true to ourselves, if we value, respect, honor, and love ourselves, we will attract the right people. The Law of Attraction says that what we put out, we get back or attract. Be yourself, be true to you and you will attract people who are like you. In doing this, you show yourself the love you deserve from you and from others.

I have come to realize that true, unwavering inner happiness is not found in external acquisitions. It is not found in the things I own, the titles I acquire, the job I have, or the people I associate with. To the people who surround me, I appear to have the perfect life. Trust me, there are many external blessings I give thanks for every day. But I've learned that happiness comes from the inside out and not from the outside in. The beautiful clothes, the gorgeous house, the two cars, the perfect job, the amazing kids, the hard-working husband, the extended family, the fun friends, the vacations, and money in the bank don't make you feel truly happy and fulfilled. True happiness and inner fulfillment are what you feel uncontrollably all the time, regardless of whether you have had a good or bad day. Happiness doesn't depend on whether the circumstances of your life on the outside are exactly the way you want them to be, true happiness is always there. It emanates from within us and can then be shared with others.

You can't search outwardly for what is missing in your life because all you really need or are searching for already exists within you—you just have to discover and uncover it. My lack of complete happiness was stemming from the lack of love for myself. Loving yourself is hard to do in a world that wants to judge you, wants you to conform to societal, cultural and familial expectations, wants to tell you what to do, what is best for you, wants to fit you into the perfection mold (the perfect wife, mother, daughter, daughter-in-law, sister, sister-in-law, friend, employee, woman). Recognizing that I was living a life of the status quo and that it was still not making me happy was hard to grasp. I now know that trying to live my life according to the status quo will never make me truly happy because we are all unique and different. How could living a common, ordinary and unexceptional life dictated by others' expectations and desires be perfect for everyone? It can't. And nor would I want it to be. I want to embrace my individuality and uniqueness.

I want to love myself, with all my quirks, edges, and per-fections (because there are no imperfections in the eyes of God). I am perfect just the way I am and living this per-fection can be hard in a world that wants to tell you to be more like they want you to be.

My true inner happiness resides in the NOW, being in this very moment, and connecting with my spirit. In that dimension there is only "NOW." There is no past, present and future as there is here on Earth. In Heaven it all exists at once, we can be here, there and anywhere all at the same time. The perfect time is NOW. Because the NOW con-nects us to God. The NOW connects us to our full and innate potential because it is where we came from and who we really are. Being in the moment means aligning yourself with the Universe and that's where happiness and uncon-ditional love can be found *all the time*. It is in that moment, "the present," when we forget about our past (even for a short while) and leave space enough for us to connect to our spirit, connect to the place where we originated from, and connect to God. Being in the moment helps me to feel amazingly blessed, clearer, happier, and more connected to the place my spirit came from before it entered its physical body here on Earth. All this leads to living a life with pur-pose, or as Wayne Dyer says, "Living a Life *on* Purpose."

When I began asking the questions I mentioned at the beginning of this chapter, when I began questioning my existence, my purpose and passion here on Earth, it was Spirit trying to find me all along. God was gently tapping on my shoulder and saying, "Teresa, there's more to your world as you know it." Living in the NOW takes conscious effort every day. It means centering myself. It means being alive with my eyes wide open. It means connecting with who I am deep within me regularly. It means reaffirming who I am inside to be able to approach each new day with renewed vigor and strength. It means I make time to give thanks for all the blessings in my life in my gratitude practice. My past helped mold me into the person I am today and living in the NOW will help me to create the reality I want in my future day by day. Today I love myself, I feel fulfilled and complete (no longer looking outside myself for who I am or for what I need) and I feel happy, truly and genuinely happy.

If you've wondered about some of these same questions, experienced degrading and demeaning situations, been hurt and/or humiliated by others, felt alone, if you're carrying your past into your present, and/or feel as though you've lost yourself in the living of your life, my hope is that you'll be inspired to follow these *steps to true inner happiness*. It's time to stop playing it small, stop trying to be someone else, and stop living your life according to external expectations. Claim your life back. Start honoring and respecting yourself by living each day as your true self, as who you were meant to be in this life and to your fullest potential. True, genuine, resolute, and unwavering happiness is within your grasp. Reach inwards and experience it! Happiness and fulfillment await you.

WELCOME TO THE DECISION TO HEAL TOOLBOX

Within the following pages you will find a series of explorations that were the very tools we each used to navigate through our own dark moments. Now we offer them to you. It is our mission to not only provide you with stories of hope, but also with the resources to help you begin your own extraordinary path from suffering to love.

This section was created to be supportive and self-guided, there is no right or wrong way to use these tools. You can simply flip through at random or just follow your heart and complete a section that speaks to you in that moment.

Don't be afraid to make a mess or have everything be precise… just be you, as you are every time you turn to these pages. Let these tools spark a sense of reverence for your own decision to heal.

In closing, we hope this book truly provides you with the understanding that you are not alone.

Thank you for allowing us to walk this path with you.

One note before you begin: If you are feeling particularly low, please know that reaching out and asking for help
isn't a sign of weakness. If you are struggling with thoughts
of suicide, we have included the numbers to the Prevention
Lifelines on page 219.

EXERCISES

LETTER TO SELF

What would you want yourself to know or say that they may not have heard yet? Use this as an opportunity to be real, truthful and honest with yourself in a new way. You may be surprised how it opens the door to more acceptance, self-love, forgiveness, compassion that may be limited or not currently present.

Dear _____,

WHAT I LOVE ABOUT MYSELF

We can often be immersed in who we are not being, what we are not doing or what we don't have in our life. What if we were to place our focus on the basic essence of our uniqueness as a person? Start off by listing 5 - 10 things you love about yourself and keep going until you decide it is enough for now.

Ex. I love that you love to have fun. I love that you love reading.

I love that you love _____

Expanding on what you love about yourself.

What I love about myself is _____?

THE TEACHINGS OF OUR STORIES

What might the stories in your life be trying to teach you? What learning can be taken away from those stories and experiences in your life in order to embrace the lessons to move forward with new perspectives? Such as gratitude, forgiveness, presence, self-acceptance, trust, belief, etc

WORTHY AND ENOUGH EXPERIENTIAL EXERCISE

Imagine a present is being given to you. Visualize the box, the size, the wrapping, the bow or any other details that stand out for you. Inside this present is love, forgiveness, compassion, acceptance, freedom, worthiness, being enough.

What do each of those look like? What do each of those feel like?

What thoughts are created? How would it feel to receive those things?

Close your eyes for a moment to take it all in. Hold those thoughts and feelings, all the feelings and thoughts that come with all these things. Now, imagine yourself having this present in your hands. Load up on the anticipation and excitement before you open it.

Remember you chose to receive this special gift as it is handed to you.

Now imagine yourself opening your gift. Unwrapping it as you visualized it.

Allow all the thoughts and feelings to be present with you when you think of love, forgiveness, compassion, acceptance, freedom, worthiness, being enough.

Hold this moment as long as you can. When it begins to fade, say "release."

Repeat this pattern 4 more times.

Everything you experience in this moment is always available to you.

This gift can never be taken away. You can open it whenever you want.

How does it feel to be worthy, enough and free?

REPLACING THE INNER CRITIC WITH COMPASSIONATE VOICE (SELF TALK SOOTHING)

I choose to forgive myself in this moment so I can love myself now and heal.

If forgiveness is a choice to feel better, I accept the choice of healing.

How can I give myself more empathy and compassion in this moment?

My life is always trying to teach me something. What I think is a failure or mistake, is an opportunity for growth and to be grateful for what I am learning.

I welcome my thoughts and feelings in this moment because they are trying to tell me something. They involve a calling of love for myself or others. I wonder what that might be?

My mind wants me to acknowledge my mistake, my heart wants to forgive me for making it. I can acknowledge it and forgive myself. Thank you for helping me grow, I forgive myself.

I acknowledge I am not perfect, and I accept that my imperfection does not impact my worthiness. It makes me human. In order to love myself now, I will be required to surrender to my suffering. Surrendering means I choose to let it go. I choose to let it go so I can love myself now. It is difficult to forgive myself in this moment. I appreciate and respect you. I will put our conversation in this box which is labeled "high priority" to discuss later when I can devote to you my full attention. What would I like to experience in this moment? I wonder what choices I can create to experience what I desire? If someone were faced with the same situation you are faced with now, take a step back and visualize what advice would you give them?

JOURNALING PROMPTS FOR SELF-REFLECTION

Reflecting on your circumstances and desires and determining whether they are authentically yours (originating from your spirit) or influenced by others (such as family, society, culture, and religion) can help you release desires that are holding you back from living your life authentically and according to your true and inner self. Reflect on the following questions and write down your responses, preferably with pen-on-paper. The process of documenting your answers has the effect of removing mental blocks and allows us to use more of our brainpower to better understand ourselves and the world around us."[1]

1. What are the circumstances and/or things (desires) that you believe will make you happy?
2. You probably have desires and are doing some things that you believe you "should" be doing and not because you really want those things. You're probably doing those things because someone else thinks it's what is best, or in order to please some-

one, or to avoid being rejected. List the things that you do because you have been brought up to believe they will make you happy, but you don't really want to do them.

3. Reflect on whether any of the above desires are influenced primarily by your society, friends, religion, culture or upbringing? If yes, which desires are they?

Are any desires listed in question one authentic desires originating from your true inner self? These desires feel natural when you do them and give you a feeling of fulfillment, contentment, joy, and happiness. These desires are those that light a spark within you and give you endless energy when you are completing them. You will also notice that desires which originate from your true inner self have more to do with "being," rather than "doing or having." These desires may also be those that you keep within yourself and are afraid to share them with others. They can be desires you feel ashamed or guilty about expressing to others. They can be the things we try to rationalize ourselves out of pursuing because we feel unworthy, less than others, or we fear humiliation and rejection. If so, what are these desires which are part of your true self?

4. Are you resisting your authentic inner desires for any of the following reasons: fear of reper-

cussions from others; guilt over hurting someone else; guilt over disappointing another; fear
of being judged; fear of being criticized; fear of
being humiliated; fear of not being enough or
worthy of those desires; fear of being rejected;
and/or fear of abandonment or being alone?

5.   Which emotions (shame, guilt, fear, etc.) are preventing you from making your authentic desires
a reality?

6.   In what ways have you limited yourself in expressing your unique talents, gifts and passions with the
people around you? Have you felt unworthy or
"not good enough" to chase those dreams or aspirations? Have you let the negative opinion of others dissuade you from doing things of interest to
you? Or perhaps you second guess yourself and
it deters you to from pursuing your goals?

7.   Making decisions for your life based on what
others believe is giving away your power and letting fear rule your life. To evaluate how much of
your power you give away, consider the reasons
you don't do what you really want to do and live
inauthentically because of it.

8.   Reflect on these possible areas in your life and
determine which of these areas you have been
giving your power away and allowing others to
control your life: what you do for a living; who
you date or marry; where you live; what you wear
or look like; how you spend your time; how you
raise your children; what you believe; what you

say; if you participate in activities which make you feel fulfilled and happy; whether or not you have what you want in life; whether or not you pursue your inner dreams and aspirations; and whether or not you reach your full potential.

9. Is there a strong correlation between the areas of your life you are unsatisfied with and the areas of your life you allow others to determine for you?

10. If you did begin taking action to make your authentic desires a reality, what would this entail? What would you need to do to make this happen in the various areas of your life?

11. It takes a lot of strength to suppress the desires which are coming from deep within ourselves in order to make others (family, culture, religion) content. It can be exhausting to pretend to be something we're not just to make those around us happy and accepting of us. If you have the strength to suppress your inner desires to 'save face', you have the strength to 'face the music' and live your authentic self. What would it take for you to begin living your authentic self and making those desires a reality?

12. Taking small steps every day to make our authentic desires a reality means respecting and honoring who we really are. This brings us closer to living our full potential and true purpose here on Earth. Are you respecting and honoring yourself in: everything that you do; the various relationships you have with others; your self-talk;

the beliefs about yourself; and how you live your life everyday?

13. Take a moment to reflect on your self-talk. Is your internal dialogue kind, gentle and loving or is it demeaning and uncompassionate?

14. Respecting and honoring ourselves first is showing ourselves the love we desire and deserve. In order for us to love others and accept the love from others, we must first love ourselves. Do you love yourself completely, just as you are? Are you able to look yourself in the mirror and say, "I love you"? If not, refer to the positive affirmations section of this workbook to begin using this practice as another possible means to assist you in getting to the place where you are able to say "yes" to the above questions. Create affirmations which provide words of support, compassion, and encouragement to yourself. If there are particular things you have difficulty accepting about yourself, use affirmations to address those things in a kind and loving way.

15. We can often compliment others with ease but find it difficult for us to do the same thing to ourselves. Shine the light on your magnificence and write down ten things you love about yourself. Give yourself permission to enjoy this moment of self-celebration. Remember that in the eyes of your true self, you are perfect and whole just as you are.

16. In what ways do you show yourself love and practice self-care?

17. Do you feel that you make time to show yourself love as often as you need it? If not, what actions can you take to make time to reconnect with yourself?

18. What activities make you feel most like your true self, alive, balanced, and at peace? Can you commit to making time for these activities every day, even if it is just for a few minutes?

19. Reflect on the times in which you have felt very connected to your true self. Would you describe these times as moments when you were "being in the NOW," or in "God's Moment"? If yes, how do you feel in those times? What does being connected to your true self in those moments feel like?

20. Gratefulness is directly correlated to happiness. The more grateful you are, the more happiness you feel. Having a gratitude practice allows you to make time to recognize the blessings in your life. Being aware of and thankful for your blessings opens your consciousness to experience miracles in your life and invite more of those miracles to occur. Consider keeping a gratitude journal where you make note of three things you felt grateful for or inspired by each day. You can also take about 5 minutes or so to reflect on things you are grateful for just as you wake up in the morning (to set positive intentions for the day) and/or just before you fall asleep at night (to bring those blessings into your subconscious mind and invite more of those blessings into your next day).

21. What messages have you been taught about creativity, especially your creativity (or the supposed lack thereof)?

22. What have you enjoyed or not enjoyed about being creative in the past—for example, creating artistic, musical, written, etc. work?

23. What do you like to do and where do you like to go to awaken a sense of joy in yourself?

24. What are some potential topics that you would be interested in creating a work about? Here are a few ideas: home, art, music, work, love, hate, healing, trauma, progress, history, abandonment, creativity.

25. Try writing, drawing, painting, singing, playing an instrument, or another form of creative expression for five minutes, timed, by hand rather than by computer, if possible. Work to keep going without editing yourself or worrying about it being "good" --go for what feels uncomfortable and have fun. Write down/record how you feel before beginning the activity and how you feel afterwards. Repeat this as much as you need to, whether or not you think the result is "good."

26. Try creating a work about who or what you love. Again, work to let go of perfectionism.

27. If you feel safe, consider sharing an original work in a supportive environment—for example, with supportive close friends or family members or at a welcoming open mic.

28. Small changes we make add up to big changes. According to psychologists, it can take approxi-

mately 21 days of conscious and consistent effort to create new habits that are self-loving and serve you. Are you willing to make a commitment to making small changes to respect and honor your true self? What small changes can you start to make every day to begin to reclaim your life?

29. Are you willing to make the necessary changes in the areas which are preventing you from living your authentic self and hindering your true inner happiness and fulfillment? Yes or no?

30. What do I really want in my life?

31. Why is that important to me and what do I think I will feel once I have it?

32. More importantly, how do I WANT to feel?

33. Become aware when you are feeling negative, frustrated, and dissatisfied energy within you and how you are acting out from those energetic spaces. Drop the judgment and allow curiosity and be truthful with yourself about what you are thinking! Really get raw and honest with yourself, and notice during these times, what am I thinking? Are these thoughts making me feel the way I desire to feel mentally, emotionally and even physically? If not, are these thoughts what I even want to be thinking and believing if they aren't creating the feelings and experiences I desire in my life?

34. How does this thought make me feel and does it serve me?

35. Do I like the way this thought makes me feel?

36. When I feel this way, what actions do I take or not take, or how do I react?

37. What results show up in my life when I am thinking these thoughts and taking these actions, inactions or reactions?

38. Are these results desirable and what I want to be creating in my life?

39. What am I believing about myself?

40. Are these beliefs what I truly want to believe about myself, or am I punishing, devaluing or victimizing myself?

41. If what I am believing makes me feel terrible, what do I want to believe instead?

42. What can I decide to believe instead that makes me feel at peace and have compassion for myself and others regardless of circumstances I cannot control, and liking my reasons for these beliefs?

[1] "Science Shows Something Surprising About People Who Still Journal." Mic. N. p., 2015. Web. 26 Aug. 2019.

POSITIVE AFFIRMATIONS

Science has proven that the use of positive affirmations works to rewire the brain by creating new neural pathways and rewriting the thoughts from negative to positive in our subconscious mind. By repeating positive statements about ourselves, neuroscience has proven that our brain begins to believe the new statements and even elicits positive physical changes in the body. The following are affirmations you can use daily and especially in moments when you feel you need to affirm your authentic self. Use them also as exemplars for creating your own affirmations around the areas you are having difficulty accepting about yourself.

1. I AM investing in me. I now understand that in order to be treated as I deserve, I must first love myself.
2. Even though I may not be loved or accepted by one, does not mean I am not loved at all.
3. I AM loved. I AM safe.
4. I will let go of fear and trust myself.
5. I deserve to be loved and happy.

6. I will not abuse my own body; I do not have to kill pain with pain. I AM kind to myself when I am upset and keep myself in great condition.

7. I AM worth my own self love and acceptance.

8. I CAN allow myself to feel my feelings and let them pass naturally without becoming anxious.

9. I accept anxiety will happen, but it doesn't have to be overwhelming, and I can breathe and find inner balance.

10. I choose to forgive myself for mistakes made and learn from each one.

11. I AM NOT a victim; I am an empowered person.

12. I have a voice.

13. I AM more than enough.

14. I accept ALL of who I am!

15. I AM healthy.

16. I AM abundant.

17. I AM love.

18. I AM peace.

19. I AM whole and perfect just as I am.

20. I AM not my past or my past mistakes.

21. I AM thankful for . . . . (blessings in your life).

22. I am enough and loveable exactly as I am.

23. It is not selfish to love myself and make myself a priority.

24. I forgive and accept myself.

25. I am not invisible without a voice; I have a powerful presence and a voice.

26. I have my own back again, and again, because I choose to trust and love myself.

27. The beauty and power are that I get to choose what I think and believe.
28. The only belief I truly need is the belief in myself.
29. I am a resilient soul warrior full of light for myself and others-I am not a victim.
30. I am worthy, deserving, lovable and enough, period.
31. True healing begins when I allow myself to fully see and know myself.
32. See with my soul, not my ego; this is liberation and pure love.

RESOURCES

RECOMMENDED READING LIST

Breaking The Habit of Being Yourself: How to Lose Your Mind and Create a New One by Dr. Joe Dispenza

Wishes Fulfilled: Mastering the Art of Manifesting by Dr. Wayne W. Dyer

Change Your Thoughts - Change Your Life: Living the Wisdom of the Tao by Dr. Wayne W. Dyer

I Can See Clearly Now by Dr. Wayne W. Dyer

E-Squared: Nine Do-It-Yourself Energy Experiments That Prove Your Thoughts Create Your Reality by Pam Grout

E-Cubed: Nine More Energy Experiments That Prove Manifesting Magic and Miracles Is Your Full-Time Gig by Pam Grout

THE DECISION TO HEAL

Self Compassion by Kristin Neff

The Gifts of Imperfection by Brene Brown

Daring Greatly by Brene Brown

Mirror Work by Louise Hay

The Power of Now by Eckhart Tolle

Words of Gratitude for Mind, Body, and Soul by Robert Emmons and Joanna Hill

Gratitude by Oliver Sacks

Man's Search For Meaning by Viktor Frankl

Happiness Now!: Timeless Wisdom for Feeling Good by Robert Holden

Lost Connections by Johann Hari

The Five Side Effects of Kindness by David R. Hamilton

The Power of Positive Thinking by Norman Vincent Peale

The Universe Has Your Back, by Gabrielle Bernstein

Judgment Detox, by Gabrielle Bernstein

Braving The Wilderness, by Brene Brown

You Are A Badass, by Jen Sincero

The Untethered Soul, by Michael A. Singer

For meditation and relaxation: Insight Timer app; Calm app: https://www.calm.com/

Breathe app: https://breethe.com/

Free resource: YouTube: Abraham Hicks/ abraham-hicks.com

HELP LINES

National Suicide Prevention Lifeline: https://suicidepreventionlifeline.org/

If you or someone you know is suicidal or in emotional distress, contact the National Suicide Prevention Lifeline. Trained crisis workers are available to talk 24 hours a day, 7 days a week. Your confidential and toll-free call goes to the nearest crisis center in the Lifeline national network. These centers provide crisis counseling and mental health referrals.

Call: 1-800-273-8255

Veterans Crisis Line: www.veteranscrisisline.net

Are you a Veteran in crisis or concerned about one? Connect with the Veterans Crisis Line to reach caring, qualified responders with the Department of Veterans Affairs. Many of them are Veterans themselves. This free support is Confidential and available every day, 24/7. It is available for All Veterans, Service members, National

Guard and Reserve and their family members and friends.

Call: 1-800-273-8255 opt. 1 or Text 838255

SAMHSA Treatment Referral Helpline: https://www.samhsa.gov/

Get general information on mental health and locate treatment services in your area. Speak to a live person, Monday through Friday from 8 a.m. to 8 p.m. EST.

Call: 1-877-SAMHSA7 (1-877-726-4727)

National Domestic Violence Hotline: https://www.thehotline.org/

Their highly trained advocates are available 24/7/365 to talk confidentially with anyone experiencing domestic violence, seeking resources or information, or questioning unhealthy aspects of their relationship.

Call: 1-800-799-7233/CHAT AVAILABLE/TTY/ESPAÑOL

Lesbian, Gay, Bisexual and Transgender (LGBT) National Hotline: https://www.glbthotline.org/

Call: 1-888-843-4564

LGBT National Youth Talkline toll-free phone:

Call: 1-800-246-PRIDE (1-800-246-7743)

LGBT National Senior Talkline toll-free phone:

Call: 1-888-234-7243

The Trevor Project / www.trevorproject.org

Their trained counselors are available to support you 24/7. If you are a young person in crisis, feeling suicidal, or in need of a safe and judgment-free place to talk, call the TrevorLifeline now Call: 1-866-488-7386

NOTES

INTRODUCTION

1. https://afsp.org/about-suicide/suicide-statistics/. Accessed Aug. 29, 2019.

2. https://www.military.com/daily-news/2019/01/30/active-duty-military-suicides-near-record-highs-2018.html. Accessed Aug. 29, 2019

3. https://adaa.org/about-adaa/press-room/facts-statistics. Accessed Aug. 29, 2019.

4. https://adaa.org/about-adaa/press-room/facts-statistics. Accessed Aug. 29, 2019.

5. https://americanspcc.org/our-voice/bullying/statistics-and-information/. Accessed Aug. 29, 2019.

6. https://www.thetrevorproject.org/resources/preventing-suicide/facts-about-suicide/. Accessed Aug. 29, 2019.

7. https://ncadv.org/statistics. Accessed Aug. 29, 2019.

AUTHOR BIOS

NICOLE SMITH

Nicole Smith is a born and raised California girl currently transplanted on the Coast of Virginia. She is a proud wife, mom, foodie and ocean lover! Nicole is also a Military Veteran turned Life Coach and Mental Wellness Advocate.

She suffered from an incredibly low self-esteem much of her life and found it impossible to love herself in order to feel "good enough" in just about every relationship. While serving our country, she silently fought a battle to remain in control of the anxiety and depression that overcame her. Finally hitting rock bottom was the breakthrough where her own transformation journey began. It was her blessing in disguise and led her to discovering her true self-worth and how to heal her life. Her path to healing transformed her so deeply that she decided to retire from her successful military career. Connecting to a new purpose, she created Navigate Your Freedom, and is now serving the military community in a new way by helping women who are burnt out from the military lifestyle to become just as committed to themselves as they are their country.

Isn't your own freedom worth navigating? To inquire about working with Nicole, Please visit: www.navigateyour-freedom.com | email: nicole@navigateyourfreedom.com

"Your story could be the key that unlocks some-one else's prison. Don't be afraid to share it."

—Toby Mac

JOSH FRIEDBERG

Josh Friedberg is a writer, essayist, scholar, music historian, tutor, storyteller, teacher, singer, and songwriter who lives in Chicago. He has won multiple awards from the Illinois Woman's Press Association's (IWPA) annual Communications Contests, including first place designations for the personal essays, online feature articles, arts & entertainment articles, and personal columns categories, as well as an Honorable Mention in the National Federation of Press Women's (NFPW) 2020 Communication Contest. He has published over thirty articles, including as a columnist at the *Good Men Project* website and contributor to *PopMatters*, the web magazine on popular culture. He holds a master's degree in English from Northeastern

Illinois University and has also been a radio DJ. In 2020, he gave a TEDx talk on creativity and disability issues. He is proudly autistic, which informs all of his work, as well as living with Bipolar Disorder, Attention Deficit Hyperactivity Disorder (ADHD), anxiety, and other disabilities, and he hopes his story inspires others to channel their creativity and know that they are not alone!

You can reach Josh at joshwritingtutor@gmail.comand connect on Twitter and Instagram@joshfrmusic.

JULIE RABORN

Julie Raborn is a Life Coach and Self-love Coach living on the freshwater coast of Lake Michigan in Traverse City, Michigan. She loves writing, traveling, hiking, kayaking, yoga, copious amounts of laughter and coffee, loving and inspiring people, and a deep love for all thing's scarves, vests and beanie caps! Throughout years of bullying and physical abuse, and self-destructive thoughts, beliefs and behaviors, she had a painful breaking point knowing she could no longer tolerate this way of being. She was suffering from extremely low self-esteem, no belief in herself or her worth, and was in a vicious cycle of self-loathing. She made the independent, powerful choice to leave her corporate job, sell her home and move away from everything and everyone she knew to live where she'd dreamt to live all her life-in Traverse City. She made a decision to have her own back and pave her path of deep exploration and healing through coaching and self-love. She chose to live by soul-led desires instead of staying stuck in fear, self-loathing and believing she was not good enough in any capacity. She discovered her pain and experiences are her gift to help others. She provides transformational coaching with the knowing there is another side to suffering and supports others to get there; the magic is on the other side of fear. She inspires others into action to finally feel better, create experiences they desire, and liberate themselves from negative self-limiting thoughts, beliefs and behaviors.

You are enough and choosing to love yourself is the missing key to having the life you desire...I'll be right by your side...you are not alone!

www.truetoyouwellnessbyjulie.com

To work with Julie, contact her at: truetoyouwellnessbyjulie@gmail.com

KRISTIN LARSEN

Kristin Larsen is a Transformational Health Coach who has certification in health coaching, life coaching and mastery transformation coaching method.

Kristin lives in Ontario, Canada, is a father of two magnificent (enough as they are) children and husband to an unconditionally loving, supportive wife.

He values and enjoys powerful conversations, smiling, laughing, personal growth, physical activity, nature, family, connection, creativity, helping others, witnessing the joy and creation by others.

He helps guide men and women to change their habits, create new mindsets so they can embrace an empowered way of living into what they envision.

He assists others to establish confidence in their body and mind so they can have clarity in their life, freedom in their thoughts, and take power in their actions.

In his practice he places focus on identifying the root cause of what is preventing or holding someone back from having what they want in their health and life.

He places importance on gradual long term habit change and accepted invitations of new mindsets to form new ways of thinking and being. He has found this helped others to create new possibilities to take empowered action towards what they want.

If you would like to follow, connect or learn more about Kristin please visit: www.klhealthcoaching.com

"No matter where you are, the first step is the most powerful action you can take!"

–Kristin Larsen
Transformational Health Coaching

KATELYN M. FLORES

Katelyn M. Flores - mover, shaker, and light seeker. Katelyn is currently living in the Northeast United States with her family and beloved fur babies. She loves creativity, all things "woo" and brings a healthy dose of sass to the table. It wasn't always that way! She is a Health and Life Coach now, AND she has walked the walk. Katelyn suffered from obesity, bullying, domestic violence, self-harm, low self-esteem, depression, and even suicidal thoughts for most of her life. Overcoming a lifetime of adversity and setbacks, Katelyn boldly up leveled her life to new heights through consistent reinvention of herself, her belief systems and the resuscitation of her powerful intuition. With fierce love and undeniable vigor and grit, she turned her broken heart into a healing vessel. In 2018, Katelyn left 13 years of social work to fearlessly follow her dreams and pursue her passion of helping people in a more intentional way, and Free Your Tangled Mind, LLC was born. Through her incredible work as a healer, she has developed a reputation as the "helper of the light seekers" and assists people in navigating through food obsession and emotional eating to lose weight, gain clarity around the root cause of their cyclical behavior, release their insecurity and begin to live a life free from obsession and pain.

Do you want to MAKE. SHIFT. HAPPEN. too? To work with Katelyn directly please visit: www.freeyourtangled-min.com | fb.me/freeYTM | email: freeyourtangled-mind@gmail.com

> *"Our deepest fear is not that we are inadequate. Our deepest fear is that we are powerful beyond measure. It is our light, not our darkness that most frightens us. We ask ourselves, Who am I to be brilliant, gorgeous, talented, fabulous? Actually, who are you not to be?"*
>
> *–Marianne Williamson*

TERESA GRECO

Teresa Greco is an educator and educational technologies consultant from Toronto, Ontario, Canada. She is the editor and senior writer at two national Canadian magazines and an author of teaching and learning resources for one of Canada's leading educational publishers. Teresa is also a wife and proud mother of two incredible children, a happiness coach, public speaker, and reiki practitioner. She has completed her Master's Degree in Education, with specializations in Technological Literacy and Special Education. An educator of over 20 years, Teresa has taught across Canada supporting students, parents, and teachers in various capacities. As an author and happiness coach, Teresa does public speaking, holds workshops, and mentors others about embracing, honoring, loving, and celebrating their true authentic self and achieving their own personal happiness and fulfillment. Teresa is working towards the launch of her own book entitled "Steps to True Happiness" and is spreading light and love with others on her website: www.teresagreco.ca, Instagram page @teresagreco_stepstohappiness and Facebook page, Steps To True Happiness With Teresa Greco.

You can also connect with Teresa by email at stepstotruehappiness@gmail.com in regard to speaking engagements, workshops, and services.

"Sometimes you have to let go of the life you thought you wanted in order to make room for the life you are truly meant for... When life takes you in an unexpected direction, trust that it is taking you closer to where you are meant to be."

–Nikki Banas

CPSIA information can be obtained
at www.ICGtesting.com
Printed in the USA
LVHW111821041022
729966LV00018B/127

9 781642 378276